Liberal Fascisms

Žižek's Essays

Series Editors: Liza Thompson and Hannah Wilks

Žižek's Essays showcase the best of Slavoj Žižek's thought and writing in short, punchy collections of essays. Carefully curated to chart the intellectual journeys of one of the world's prominent philosophers, each book brings together writings addressing the most urgent issues facing the contemporary subject. Written with Žižek's characteristic verve, expansiveness, erudition and imagination, the essays combine the enduring Žižekian preoccupations of Marxism, psychoanalysis, contemporary politics and film with emerging themes – particle physics, new theories of history, authenticity in the age of AI, war and ecological collapse in all its catastrophic forms. *Žižek's Essays* invite both seasoned readers and new discoverers to experience thinking life, politics and history through the idiosyncratic and topsy-turvy brilliance of the ultimate philosopher for a world turned upside down.

Also Available from Bloomsbury

Zero Point, *Slavoj Žižek*
Against Progress, *Slavoj Žižek*
Christian Atheism, *Slavoj Žižek*
Freedom, *Slavoj Žižek*
Surplus-Enjoyment, *Slavoj Žižek*
Hegel in a Wired Brain, *Slavoj Žižek*
Sex and the Failed Absolute, *Slavoj Žižek*
Disparities, *Slavoj Žižek*
Antigone, *Slavoj Žižek*

Liberal Fascisms

Slavoj Žižek

BLOOMSBURY ACADEMIC
LONDON • NEW YORK • OXFORD • NEW DELHI • SYDNEY

BLOOMSBURY ACADEMIC

Bloomsbury Publishing Plc, 50 Bedford Square, London, WC1B 3DP, UK
Bloomsbury Publishing Inc, 1359 Broadway, New York, NY 10018, USA
Bloomsbury Publishing Ireland, 29 Earlsfort Terrace, Dublin 2, D02 AY28, Ireland

BLOOMSBURY, BLOOMSBURY ACADEMIC and the Diana logo are trademarks
of Bloomsbury Publishing Plc

First published in Great Britain 2026

Copyright © Slavoj Žižek, 2026

Slavoj Žižek has asserted his right under the Copyright, Designs and Patents Act,
1988, to be identified as Author of this work.

Design: Ben Anslow
Photo © jeromefavrestudio

All rights reserved. No part of this publication may be: i) reproduced or
transmitted in any form, electronic or mechanical, including photocopying,
recording or by means of any information storage or retrieval system without
prior permission in writing from the publishers; or ii) used or reproduced in
any way for the training, development or operation of artificial intelligence (AI)
technologies, including generative AI technologies. The rights holders expressly
reserve this publication from the text and data mining exception as per Article
4(3) of the Digital Single Market Directive (EU) 2019/790.

Bloomsbury Publishing Plc does not have any control over, or responsibility for,
any third-party websites referred to or in this book. All internet addresses given
in this book were correct at the time of going to press. The author and publisher
regret any inconvenience caused if addresses have changed or sites have
ceased to exist, but can accept no responsibility for any such changes.

A catalogue record for this book is available from the British Library.

A catalog record for this book is available from the Library of Congress.

ISBN: PB: 978-1-3505-7316-1
       ePDF: 978-1-3505-7317-8
       eBook: 978-1-3505-7318-5

Series: Žižek's Essays

Typeset by RefineCatch Limited, Bungay, Suffolk
Printed by Integrated Books International, United States of America

For product safety-related questions contact productsafety@bloomsbury.com.

To find out more about our authors and books visit
www.bloomsbury.com and sign up for our newsletters.

Contents

Introduction: From the Standpoint of Eternity	1
Part 1. The Global Mess We're In	15
Altona, Los Angeles: From the Nearby to the Neighbour	17
The Ambivalence of De-commodification	23
Decolonization and the Public Use of Reason	28
Let It Rot …	37
Re-staging the Event	45
Part 2. Local Turbulences	51
Dark Humour in the Reign of Daddy Cool	53
Next Year in Gaza!	63
Sumud: Remember This Word	70
Peace for Our Time	75
The Story of Three Faces	86
Part 3. The Black Hole of Our World	93
Let's Pray Trump Survives	95
Grab 'em by the Pussy	107
Why Evil Men Need Noble Spirits	122
Donald Trump as a Gramscian	135
Mamdani's Wager	141
Conclusion: Abandon All Hope, You Who Enter Radical Politics	145
Notes	158
Index	179

Introduction
From the Standpoint of Eternity

In 2009, when political correctness still reigned supreme, Jonah Goldberg published *Liberal Fascism*,[1] a book which claimed the true heirs to fascism were actually progressive liberals. Goldberg argued that the most insidious attempts to control our lives (such as smoking bans and pervasive surveillance from security cameras) originated from the Left. To support his thesis that it was modern progressivism, not conservatism, which shared the same intellectual roots as Fascism, Goldberg cited examples including the Clinton personality cult, the military chic of 1960s student radicals, and what he called Hollywood's totalitarian aesthetics (today, he would certainly adduce cancel culture, wokeism, DEI policies and growing acceptance and rights for LGBT+ people, as well). My thesis throughout this text is almost exactly the opposite of Goldberg's: to paraphrase Max Horkheimer, who wrote in 1939 that 'Whoever is not willing to talk about Capitalism should also keep quiet about Fascism', I would argue that 'whoever is not willing to talk (critically) about liberalism should also keep quiet about fascism'. And, perhaps, also about Donald Trump.

These writings are not about Trump. However, the myriad issues interrogated in these essays are all in dialogue with the historical *event* that is the second term of Trump's presidency – an event in the catastrophic sense of an occurrence which makes us aware that our world, as we knew it, has ended. The shortest formal definition of such an event is one that doesn't only change the specific circumstances of a situation, but changes the very co-ordinates of the situation itself. I can illustrate this best with an updated version of an old joke from the GDR (German Democratic Republic) that I have told many times: Putin, Xi and Trump meet God and each is allowed to ask him a question. Putin begins: 'Tell me, what will happen to Russia in the next few decades?' God answers: 'Russia will gradually become a colony of China.' Putin turns away, appalled, and starts to cry. Xi asks his question: 'And what will happen to China in the next few decades?' God answers: 'The Chinese economic miracle will be over, and China will have to return to a hardline dictatorship to survive while asking Taiwan for help.' Xi, too, turns away in horror and begins to weep. Finally, Trump asks: 'And what will be the fate of the US after I take over again?' In response, God himself turns away and starts to cry ... This is the true change, when God – who stands here for the big Other, the neutral frame that encompasses the situation – breaks down. Trump's second term constitutes, of course, just such a total rupture, a catastrophic event: the basic co-ordinates with which we map and measure the quality of public life no longer steady or orient us. 'Normal' standards are suspended and all categories and expectations will have to be thoroughly remade.

Such a fracture also has its positive side: it compels us to finally accept the fact that there is no going back to the old era of the liberal-democratic paternalistic state. We are catapulted out of the denial and bargaining to which we have been clinging for so long, into acceptance and the blunt fact of defeat. A new beginning from the zero point is needed.[2]

The Left's inability to accept that things have changed, catastrophically and forever, has been symptomatic of its failure to combat the new populism which Trump exemplifies. It also, perhaps, speaks of the intellectual laziness which the Left, especially the liberal Left, all too often displays: when a new and terrifying phenomenon emerges; instead of analyzing it closely with an open mind and trying to understand its nature and origin, they quickly condemn it, immediately invoking the one truly bad label in politics, 'fascism'. But surely it isn't enough, either as a political tactic or as a tool for understanding how this catastrophe happened, to simply brand Trumpian populism as a new form of fascism. Trump is not just authoritarian. His dream is to allow the market to function freely at its most destructive, from brutal profiteering to dismissing all ethical limitations in public media (against sexism and racism) as a form of socialism.

The new populist Right wants to annihilate all the phenomena targeted by Goldberg, perceiving them as signs of a new Leftist totalitarianism; but the result is, as we can see after the first months of Trump's second term as president, a massive increase and emboldening of state intervention, control and censorship. The new populist Right treats Communism and corporate capitalism as the same – but the true identity of the opposites resides elsewhere. At the beginning of Trump's first term, I was criticized for claiming that Trump was a 'pure' liberal – how could I ignore the fact that Trump was a dictatorial fascist? My critics missed the point: perhaps the best characterization of Trump is that he *is* liberal, namely a *fascist* liberal. He is the ultimate proof that liberalism and fascism work together, that they are the two sides of the same coin.

A word on terminology: the word 'liberalism' as it is used in the US has two main senses. (In Europe and the UK, this distinction is not so clear.) It can mean progressive liberalism (affirmative action, LGBT+ rights, etc.) or it can mean what they call libertarianism (the unconditional assertion of individual freedoms, rejecting progressive liberalism). It's not enough to label one liberalism 'good' and one 'bad', according to your political persuasion, and to claim that your preferred form is what liberalism 'really' is and the rest can be discarded and ignored. Progressive liberalism and libertarianism are closely interlinked, mutually interdependent; they function as the two aspects of the immanent tension that characterizes the notion of freedom. They render palpable the contradiction that inheres to the very notion of freedom.[3] Moreover, there is a difference between the US and western Europe with regard to liberalism: in most of western Europe, liberalism stands for a centrist pragmatic stance opposed to the authoritarian Right but also to the radical Left, while in the US, liberalism is perceived as progressive, even Leftist.

While I am critical of progressive liberalism and of libertarianism alike, my target in this volume is libertarianism and its fascist potential. I have opted strategically to name this 'liberal fascism', a term which at least evokes the contradictory nature of Trumpian populism. Maybe a more adequate term would be 'fascist libertarianism' since it enacts the shift of fascism from subject to predicate, as well as nailing down liberalism as libertarianism. What I hope to convey is that what we are getting with Trump today is not fascism with a liberal mask, but liberalism brought to its (fascist) conclusion, to the actualization of its hidden immanent potentials. Moreover, we should bear in mind that there are multiple forms of fascism arising today – are countries like Modi's India, Putin's Russia and Erdoğan's Turkey not also versions of authoritarian capitalism which strongly resemble fascism?

In May 2025, the BBC reported that Russian bookstores had received an official letter with a list of thirty-seven titles that should immediately be removed from the shelves. This list 'included texts by Slovenian philosopher Slavoj Žižek, Japanese novelist Ryu Murakami, and a number of Russian writers'.[4] Nice – at least I'm taken seriously! The only enigmatic thing was that one of the books mentioned – the Russian translation of *Žižek's Jokes* – is my most apolitical work! However, I recently read about a new trend among the newly-born Christian fundamentalists in the US: many of them go through their personal library and throw away writings reminding them of their Leftist youth. The report mentioned a middle-age woman, Jenny, who a few years previously went through her books 'to remove some final remnants of her left-leaning twenties: the Frankfurt school, the situationists, Žižek. She burned them.'[5] I see in this weird coincidence of book-burning and censorship the confirmation that, in spite of their conflicts, Trump's US and Putin's Russia follow the same neo-fascist trend. Since fascism is a project of conservative modernization, the tension between the modern capitalist dynamic and the traditional social order is inscribed into it. In this sense Trump *is* fascist, but with a twist: his modernization remains liberal, legitimizing itself as a defence of individual freedoms against the oppressive state. What makes Trump fascist is the fact that these 'freedoms' ultimately amount to the freedom of neo-feudal masters to exploit the poor more than ever. This techno-feudal sphere reaches well beyond GAFAM (Google, Amazon, Facebook, Apple and Microsoft): it comprises the intersection between the 'deep state' and new corporations.

The essays in this collection expound upon different aspects of liberal fascism, from economy and politics to ideology, often looking beyond the Trumpian populism of the US to western Europe, the Middle East, China, Russia and even Serbia. They are divided into three parts, which generally correspond to the triad of the universal, particular and singular: our global predicament; Europe, the Middle East, China, Africa . . .; Trump's US. To be frank, what permeates all of them is intermingled fascination and disgust. I hope this disgust doesn't blur my analysis but renders it even more acute. There is a disgust which fascinates us, secretly attracts us, and thus immobilizes us – many analyses of Trump fall into this category. But there is also a disgust we feel when we notice the chains that constrain our 'freedoms', and this disgust makes us move, act – as Rosa Luxembourg put it, 'those who do not move, do not notice their chains'.

These chains are not only those imposed by the big Enemy, the global capitalist order; they are also the chains that the long and painful process of emancipation imposed on its own agents. What was later perceived as 'Stalinist oppression' had already begun during Lenin's time in control. One should bear in mind that the first wave of anti-intellectual purges in 1922–23 – in which hundreds were put on the so-called 'Philosophers' Steamers' and exiled, mostly to Germany – coincided precisely with the imposition of the 'New Economic Policy', when restrictions were loosened on private enterprise in order to prevent hunger. The idea was that the NEP would create a new bourgeoisie which would look for its ideological support among intellectuals who were not faithfully following the party line. The purge was thus largely an act of prevention: not a punishment for what someone had done but a punishment for what someone might do in the near future. Such a perception of the situation is clearly grounded in the logic of linear progress and is best exemplified by Stalin's 'On Dialectical and Historical Materialism' (1938) where he writes that in the 1880s,

> the proletariat in Russia constituted an insignificant minority of the population, whereas the individual peasants constituted the vast majority of the population. But the proletariat was developing as a class, whereas the peasantry as a class was disintegrating. And just because the proletariat was developing as a class the Marxists based their orientation on the proletariat. And they were not mistaken; for, as we know, the proletariat subsequently grew from an insignificant force into a first-rate historical and political force.[6]

Seen this way, the proletarian revolution becomes just one in a series of systemic substitutions, replacements of an old system by a new, more progressive system. Just as slavery replaced the primitive communal system and capitalism replaced feudalism, the socialist system replaced the capitalist system:

> The slave system would be senseless, stupid and unnatural under modern conditions. But under the conditions of a disintegrating primitive communal system, the slave system is a quite understandable and natural phenomenon, since it represents an advance on the primitive communal system. [...] The demand for a bourgeois-democratic republic when tsardom and bourgeois society existed, as, let us say, in Russia in 1905, was a quite understandable, proper and revolutionary demand; for at that time a bourgeois republic would have meant a step forward. But now, under the conditions of the U.S.S.R., the demand for a bourgeois-democratic republic would be a senseless and counterrevolutionary demand; for a bourgeois republic would be a retrograde step compared with the Soviet republic.[7]

The ultimate irony is that if we measure progress in this way, then the old ironic quip that socialism is a passage from a lower to a higher state of capitalism fully holds true – in the same way that the 1968 student protests in Paris and elsewhere turned out to be a passage from more traditional to postmodern capitalism.[8]

This is where the Left fails today.[9] In contrast to its professed respect for *other* local ethnic groups, the Left as a rule speaks from an abstract rootless global position; its 'way of life' is predominantly that of the 'talking classes' (academia, mainstream and legacy media). As a result, its representative from, say, the UK has more in common with its representative from Germany or France than either has with people directly around them. For them, any mention of local roots is either constrained to *other* marginal groups (indigenous peoples, Blacks, etc.) or it is dismissed as 'fascist' – and the new populist Right is exploiting this limitation in an extremely efficient way. What this means is that the Left should reappropriate the very motif it refuses to apply to itself – local roots, ways of life, communities and grassroots politics ... 'Fascism' contains elements that can easily be made into a key moment of the Communist vision. Crazy as it may sound, *fascism also works as ersatz-Communism* – this is how one should read Walter Benjamin's claim that behind every fascism there is a failed revolution. To put it in an even more crazy way, the Left can only be saved by what it misreads as fascism.

An obvious counter-argument: but is there not a clear opposition between a way of life that refers to local roots and today's explosive digitalization where tens of millions are in daily contact through Zoom, etc.? What do local roots mean in a world where Samsung, the biggest and best-known South Korean company, moved almost all of its production to Texas, where Amazon is moving its headquarters to Gdansk in Poland? I think it is wrong to conclude from this opposition that local ways of life have lost their meaning. On the contrary, the lesson of globalization is that, since in the global economy the role of nation-states is diminishing, a new space is opening up for local cultures, from Wales to the Basque country. Our critique of Trump and Musk should be that their economic measures produce the exact opposite of what they claim: artificially created 'digital states' which obliterate all roots in tradition. Only a new Left can save and redeem (what is worth saving in) our traditions. We should also fully endorse here the insight of Claude Levi-Strauss, who pointed out how each traditional local culture sees itself as somehow superior to others, as a direct embodiment of what 'being human' means (many ancient tribes designate themselves with their term for 'human') – this 'racism' has nothing to do with modern racism proper.

This is why the idea that the Western world was so shaken by the Nazi Holocaust, not simply because it killed millions of Jews but because it applied the mass murder practised extensively by European colonizers in non-European nations on Europeans themselves, is deeply problematic. It underestimates the specifically industrial and choreographed character of the Holocaust, and this character implies the worldlessness of the global capitalist-technological society. Today's global society is no longer 'Eurocentric', it is no longer grounded in a specific cultural or ideological horizon. But why should we not take this 'worldlessness' as an open space soliciting us to build or resuscitate new multipole local worlds destined to coexist, with no need to impose themselves as 'global'?

One can easily imagine this worldless global medium not as capital but as a post-capitalist AI smoothly functioning as what Marx called the 'kingdom of necessity'. In this vision of Communism, the spiritual kingdom of freedom and the kingdom of necessity are not united in some kind of utopian synthesis where work becomes pleasure but are, rather, kept strictly apart, in contrast to what Marx called 'prehistory' where the two dimensions are falsely united (hard compulsive work is mystified into spiritual fulfilment).

This book may often give the appearance of analysing our current critical situation *sub species aeternitatis* – from the standpoint of eternity, as Spinoza put it. It disrupts general notions not only of human history and ethics but also what being-human means and what the nature of reality is. However, at the same time, it proceeds in the exact opposite way: it deals with general ontological and ethical notions *sub species actualtatis*, from the standpoint of our unique predicament, of what Walter Benjamin called *Jetzt-Zeit*, the 'now' of a singular situation in which our universal destiny is at stake. We live in an era (of global warming, of the unchecked proliferation of AI, of the threat of military self-destruction) which compels us to redefine even the most abstract philosophical notions. This is what Hegel meant by 'concrete universality': a unique historical situation is never just an example of general laws, but redefines universality itself.

Since the observation of reality *sub species aeternitatis* is the task of philosophy, breaking the spell of Trumpian populism involves much more than a shift in the political space of the US. Without exaggeration, we can say that it concerns the survival of philosophy as opposed to demagogic sophistry. So what is philosophy at its most basic?

Alain Badiou begins his *True Life* with the provocative claim that, from Socrates onward, the function of philosophy is to *corrupt the youth*, to extricate them from the predominant ideologico-political order. Such 'corruption' is needed most urgently today, in our liberal-permissive West where most people are even not aware of the way the establishment controls them precisely when they appear to be free – the most dangerous unfreedom is the unfreedom that we experience as freedom, or, as Goethe put it two centuries ago: 'None are more hopelessly enslaved than those who falsely believe they are free.' Is a libertarian, who works to destroy the thick social network of customs which make his thriving possible, really free?

The Socratic revolution was characterized by two features. First, it was a reaction to a general crisis in Greek social life which, for Socrates, was embodied by the widespread popularity of sophists, performers of empty rhetorical tricks who enacted the decay of the *polis* tradition. Secondly, what Socrates opposed to this decay was not a simple return to the glorious past but a radical self-questioning. The basic Socratic praxis is the endless repetition of the formula: 'What, exactly, do you mean by . . .?' – by virtue, truth, the Good and similar basic notions. Today, we need to subject the fundamentals of our thinking to the same questioning: what do we mean by equality, freedom, human rights, 'the people', solidarity, emancipation and all the other words we use to legitimize our decisions? Doing this thinking means that, when we are confronted with the ecological crisis, we don't just focus on saving nature, we also ask ourselves what nature means today. Encountering the rise of AI, it is not enough to ask whether machines are able to think; we should also ask what human thinking really means. We should follow in Descartes' footsteps here: when he wrote that God could have decided that one plus one does not equal two, this insight is not a regression to obscurantism but the beginning of modern science which realizes the contingency of our even most self-evident truths.

Let's give a simple but extreme case of what this Socratic thinking means. On 12 June 2025, the Air India Flight 171 from Ahmedabad in India to London Gatwick crashed thirty-two seconds after takeoff. As the aircraft reached its maximum recorded airspeed of 180 knots (330 km/h; 210 mph) three seconds after takeoff, both the fuel control switches sequentially moved from RUN to CUTOFF, one second apart. Both engines immediately shut down and stopped producing thrust. All twelve crew members and 229 of the 230 passengers aboard died. On the ground, nineteen people were killed and sixty-seven others were seriously injured. The subsequent investigation drew a chilling conclusion: the cause of the catastrophe was neither personal (pilot's error) nor mechanical but purely digital. Because of some miscommunication between the different parts of its technology, the digital system that regulates the plane was simultaneously informed that it was still on the ground and that it was already in the air; when confronted with such contradictory information, the digital system 'played it safe', just as a human might do upon seeing a machine malfunction – not knowing what was really happening, or whether the plane was on the ground or in the air, it decided to stop the machine working. It also prevented intervention by the pilots because it 'thought' that one of them might accidentally push the fuel control button. In short, the catastrophe was caused by the very precautionary measures taken to prevent a catastrophe. What the digital system was not able to do was make a simple *decision* that even a bad pilot could have taken: visually observing that the plane was in the air and switching the fuel control to RUN. The logical protocols of the digital system could not replicate the human ability to receive and act on direct sensory input, leading to a nightmarish tragedy to which we should nevertheless react by questioning how our unexamined assumptions about what 'thinking' is might have contributed.

Here, we should contrast the model of Socratic questioning with the Confucian 'rectification of names'. Confucius' analysis of the lack of connection between things and their names grounds the need to overcome this lack:

> If language is not correct, then what is said is not what is meant; if what is said is not what is meant, then what must be done remains undone; if this remains undone, morals and art will deteriorate; if justice goes astray, people will stand about in helpless confusion. Hence there must be no arbitrariness in what is said.[10]

In clear contrast to this stance, the Socratic tradition is fully aware that to really think means to think in language against language and, in this way, to destroy the ideology inscribed into our language.

Democritus, the pre-Socratic atomist, had already taken recourse to a wonderful neologism: *den*. The Ancient Greeks had two words for nothing, *medel* and *ouden*, which stand for two types of negation: *ouden* is a factual negation, something that is not but could have been; *meden* is, on the contrary, something that in principle cannot be. From *meden* we get to *den*, not simply by negating the negation in *meden*, but by displacing negation, or, rather, by supplementing negation with a subtraction. That is to say, we arrive at *den* when we take away from *meden*, not the whole negating prefix, but only its first two letters: *meden* is *med'hen*, the negation of *hen* (one): not-one. Democritus arrives at *den* by leaving out only 'me' and thus creating a totally artificial word den. *Den* is thus not nothing without 'no'; not a thing, but an 'othing', a something but still within the domain of nothing, like an ontological living dead, a spectral nothing-appearing-as something. Or, as Lacan put it: 'Nothing, perhaps? No-perhaps nothing, but not nothing.' As Heinz Wisman put it concisely: 'being is a privative state of non-being', i.e., being emerges as *othing*, by way of subtracting something from nothing.[11]

This is how you think in language against language. It is crucial to note how, contrary to the late Wittgensteinian thrust towards ordinary language, towards language as part of a life-world, materialism begins with violating the rules of ordinary language, by thinking against language. Today, the true anti-Platonist sophist is, of course, Donald Trump. On the very first page of his *Republic*, Plato wonderfully portrays how the Trumpian populists (here represented by Polemarchus) treat their opponents (here represented by Socrates, the narrator):

> Polemarchus said to me: 'I perceive, Socrates, that you and your companion are already on your way to the city.' 'You are not far wrong', I said. 'But do you see', he rejoined, 'how many we are?' 'Of course.' 'And are you stronger than all these? for if not, you will have to remain where you are.' 'May there not be the alternative', I said, 'that we may persuade you to let us go?' 'But can you persuade us, if we refuse to listen to you?', he said. 'Certainly not', replied Glaucon. 'Then we are not going to listen; of that you may be assured.'[12]

The stance of simply not listening to your opponent (if you are stronger than him) is what we encounter today again and again in big politics – and even in philosophy. One of the standard critiques of Hegel is that the notion of dialectical progress presupposes the urge to go on thinking, to bring out every consequence of a specific thought or stance: if you are an ascetic, say, thinking about it will make you realize that asceticism is an egotist stance – you are totally focused on yourself, trying desperately to erase all remainders of pleasure and joy ... But Hegel knows this: at the very beginning of his *Logic* which analyses the logical order of pure categories of thinking without any empirical presuppositions, he points out that logic is nonetheless grounded in an (ultimately contingent) act of will, a wilful decision to think. An ascetic individual can simply say: 'OK, I am really an egotist, but I don't care about it, I refuse to think what my asceticism implies, I just accept that this is what I am.'

This refusal to listen and/or to think is not just one big primordial decision; it takes place continuously in our lives. Those who support Israel simply ignore all the obvious arguments that a genocide is happening there, dismissing them as anti-Semitic lies. A similar refusal to think happens to me again and again: when I recently listed arguments for the urgency and reality of our environmental crisis,[13] the reply I got was a variation on 'We are not going to listen; of that you may be assured', and the brief explanation was that the struggle against global warming was a campaign motivated by dark reasons (destroying the prosperous West). Along these lines, Trump said in his speech at the UN General Assembly on 23 September 2025 that climate change was 'the greatest con job ever perpetrated on the world'.[14] This stance is grounded in a precise notion of justice, articulated early in the *Republic* by Thrasymachus who says: 'I proclaim that justice is nothing else than the interest of the stronger.' And he goes on to explain how

> the different forms of government make laws democratic, aristocratic, tyrannic, with a view to their several interests; and these laws, which are made by them for their own interests, are the justice which they deliver to their subjects, and him who transgresses them they punish as a breaker of the law, and unjust. In all states there is the same principle of justice, which is the interest of the government; and as the government must be supposed to have power, the only reasonable conclusion is, that everywhere there is one principle of justice, which is the interest of the stronger.[15]

Is this not, again, Trumpian politics at its purest? Is this not the justice Trump brings to the Middle East, to Ukraine …? And Trump is not alone here. On 3 July 2025, Chinese Foreign Minister Wang Yi reportedly told the European Union's top diplomat that Beijing could not accept Russia losing its war against Ukraine 'as this could allow the United States to turn its full attention to China', contradicting Beijing's public position of neutrality in the conflict. An official briefed on the talks said that the private remarks 'suggested Beijing might prefer a protracted war in Ukraine that keeps the United States from focusing on its rivalry with China'.[16] Illusions about China – the idea that, in spite of all its problematic features, it wants peace and global cooperation, and even follows some notion of justice – have been irrevocably shattered. China has made it clear that it wants a long, devastating war destroying an entire country to continue because peace could hurt its economic interests. Such brutal reasoning displayed in public is rather something one would expect from Trump ...

One conclusion to be drawn from all of this is that today we need philosophy more than ever – we need it to survive as humans. Naive as it may sound, we cannot survive without some notion of justice that transcends pragmatic considerations of survival. We have to ask ourselves what we mean when we talk about 'justice' – and what it is possible for justice to mean today.

Part 1. The Global Mess We're In

Altona, Los Angeles: From the Nearby to the Neighbour

Europe as an emancipatory idea died in Canada and almost nobody noticed. Amidst the chaotic tumult of the summer of 2025, on 16 June 2025, the Group of Seven (G7) countries, meeting for their fifty-first summit, issued a joint statement urging 'de-escalation' on Iran as tensions in the Middle East continued to rise. The G7 statement claimed that Israel had 'the right to defend itself' and asserted that 'Iran can never have a nuclear weapon'.[1] So in this formulation, de-escalation means the 'unconditional surrender' of one side (Iran). Even if it is true that Iran instigated attacks on Israel by Hamas, Hezbollah and the Houthis, what was it that opened up space for Iran to act like this? Was it not the Israeli terror against Palestinians? There are no words in the G7 statement about what we, in our naivety, were hoping for: a collective recognition of a Palestinian state and condemnation of the ongoing genocide in Gaza and the ethnic cleansing on the West Bank. The obscenity peaked with the German Chancellor, Friedrich Merz, who stated in an interview for German TV: 'This is the dirty work Israel is doing for all of us. We are also victims of this [Iranian] regime.'[2] In Gaza and on the West Bank, Israel is arguably doing the same dirty work for us –what kind of civilization needs quite so much 'dirty work', genocide included, to be done on their behalf? Merz's comments here chime with those made by Western sympathizers with Hitler, who also claimed that, by destroying the Jews and attacking the Soviet Union, he was just doing the dirty work for us, so we should publicly condemn him but silently count on him to finish the job.

Europe's demise was sealed not by some 'Oriental' despotism (as some predicted) but by the new Rightist populism whose personification is Donald Trump. A Slovene painter said in a recent interview that 'the power of the artist resides in the slightly crazy obsession to do what he believes in'.[3] Yes, that's why Goebbels claimed that Hitler was an artist whose work of art was Germany[4] – and does the same obsession not also characterize Trump, even as he encounters increasing trouble in his own artistic endeavours?

As international conflicts continue to proliferate, Trump has begun to emerge as a kind of UN peacemaker, preaching negotiations and constraint, and thereby reduced to the role of an impotent observer respectfully ignored by the aggressive participants in the actual conflicts (Russia, Israel). His mask of a neutral negotiator is, of course, utterly fake since it is always clear where he really stands (while advising Israel to show constraint in Iran, he simultaneously demanded that the USA directly supported Israel in reducing Tehran to ashes). The tension between Republican hawks and MAGA isolationists was not 'the internal war that could decide Trump's Iran response',[5] but it is a tension that defines Trump's global politics: America as local superpower ignoring the big world (MAGA isolationism) and America as global superpower intervening everywhere (classic American interventionism).

Alenka Zupančič[6] draws attention to how the Trumpian populist Right systematically takes recourse to the rhetorical figure of castration, not in the refined Lacanian sense of symbolic castration as a renunciation/deprivation which is the obverse of empowerment, i.e., which enables the subject to act with authority, but in a much more primitive imaginary sense of 'emasculation', 'feminization', etc.

What pervades the populist discourse is the threat of immediate empirical loss of power, of our masculine vitality and enjoyment. However, this threat emanates from the others (immigrants, sexual minorities, etc.) who are themselves perceived as weak and impotent. The paradox is that these others are attacked by populists not because of their strength but because of their supposed weakness and helplessness: in this logic, their weakness is contagious and threatens to infect 'us'. This paradox explains the way the extreme Right appropriates the term 'freedom of speech' – not as the right of citizens to publicly speak the truth and criticize those in power, not as the protection of critical voices, but primarily as the *right to enjoyment*: in the populist discourse, the 'loss of the freedom of speech' amounts to the impossibility to freely offend others, to utter publicly whatever pops into my mind. On 16 June 2025, as the

US–UK trade deal was signed off, Trump said the UK was protected from tariffs 'because I like them'[7] – even big economic decisions are justified by the simple contingent fact of liking a place, of enjoying being their ally . . .[8] And the killing of foreign leaders obeys the same logic of caprice: 'We know exactly where the so-called "Supreme Leader" is hiding. He is an easy target, but is safe there – we are not going to take him out, at least not for now.'[9]

The cancel culture criticized by the populist Right is thus perceived by them as the weapon used by the weak to 'castrate' the vitality of the strong (of ourselves). Here, we see the populist perversion of class struggle, in which the true class struggle is the one between 'ordinary' (masculine) American workers and the weak intruders mobilized by big corporations and the 'deep state' to emasculate the working class. It is within this logic that a Trump sympathizer can assert that 'taxpayers subsidize[d] LA riots through California's "protest-industrial complex"'.[10] Instantly recognizable in this claim is the familiar Fascist tactic of bracketing together polarized classes under the unifying label of 'enemy', as in 'Bolshevik-plutocratic plot' (for the Nazis, their war was the war 'against the alliance of bolshevism and plutocracy').[11] A similar logic of the coincidence of opposites sustains Steve Bannon's 'lesson' for Israeli Jews:

> People in Israel gotta understand something: The number one enemy to the people in Israel are American Jews that do not support Israel and do not support MAGA. The evangelical Christians and the traditional Catholics in this country have Israel's back. They have the Jews' back. The single biggest enemy to the Jewish people are not the Islamic supremacists. The biggest enemy you have is inside the wire: progressive Jewish billionaires that are funding all this stuff.[12]

As Emily Tamkin pointed out, 'this is a new twist on an old antisemitic classic: insisting that Jews are enemies from within, perpetual foreigners, outsiders even when we're insiders, incapable of belonging and of loyalty to a society'.[13] This is the practice of ideological hegemony at its purest: bringing together Zionist Jews and anti-Semitic Christians. The populist Gramscians subtly mobilize the Christian notion of 'the neighbour' ('Love thy neighbour as thyself', etc.). This neighbour is not merely a fellow human: fellow humans are friends, members of my family, co-workers, those whom I think I know intimately. A fellow human transforms themself into a neighbour when I detect in them a feature or a gesture which makes them total strangers to me: 'How could he do *that*? I never expected this from him. Is he one of us at all or an alien monster?'

It is in his account of the monstrosity of the neighbour that Lacan applies to the neighbour the term 'Thing' (*das Ding*), used by Freud to designate the ultimate object of our desires in its unbearable intensity and impenetrability. One should hear in this term all the connotations of horror fiction: the neighbour is the (evil) thing which potentially lurks beneath every familiar human face. Just think about Stephen King's *The Shining*, in which the father, a modest failed writer, gradually turns into a murderous beast who, with an evil grin, proceeds to slaughter his entire family. But the figure of the neighbour also implies the possibility of an unexpectedly positive surprise: a fellow human whom we considered just another ordinary person who displays an unexpected courage or honesty.

In Hamburg, a big city in northern Germany, there are three long-distance railway stations quite close to each other: the main station (Hamburg-Hauptbanhof), Hamburg-Dammtor and Hamburg-Altona. All three are on the same line. The seeming irrationality of having another station (Dammtor) which is just a short walk from the main station is, in fact, quite easy to explain by the class logic prevailing at the time: the ruling class wanted a station where its members could board the train unperturbed by the press of the lower-class crowd. More enigmatic is the third station – Altona. The fact is that, from the early sixteenth century, citizens of Hamburg have continuously complained about this small, originally Danish, settlement north-west of the city centre. It is not clear where the name 'Altona' originated. According to some sources, it refers to the fact that the Danish settlement was perceived as standing '*all to nah*' ('all too near') to Hamburg itself; the more probable explanation for it is '*all ten au*', 'by the brook'. However, with regard to the 'all too near' theory, one should repeat the old Italian proverb, *se non e vero, e ben' trovato* – even if it is not true [at the level of facts], it is well-founded!

This is how a symptom is organized for Freud: as a hysterical accusation which, at a basic factual level, is clearly not true, but is nonetheless 'well-founded' insofar as an unconscious desire resonates within it.

It is deeply ironic that Hamburg, arguably the most open and tolerant city in Germany, came to exemplify this structure: the symbolic function of the third station, Altona, is to keep the intruders who are always 'all too near' at a proper distance, but it also serves to displace and mystify the basic social antagonism (class struggle) into the fake antagonism between 'us' (our nation, in which all classes are united in the same social body) and 'them' (the foreign intruders). The neighbour is, by definition, always 'all too near', and Trumpian populism endeavours to forcefully assert the space of the nearby by way of projecting the uncanny dimension of the neighbour onto foreign intruders. 'Nearby' is thus given a racist twist: it should be recreated through the exclusion of (sexual, ethnic, religious) others. For Israel, Arabs are by definition 'all too near', not just in Gaza or on the West Bank but even in a distant Iran, so they have to be ruthlessly pursued and destroyed. This, of course, implies no pro-Iranian bias: the Iranian theocratic regime also mobilized its forces against the 'all too near' Israel in order to obfuscate its own class struggle, the large protests triggered by the murder of Mahsa Amini which almost toppled the regime.

Perhaps we can shed some further light onto Bannon's twisted fantasies by introducing the notion of 'the nearby' as a critical lens through which to analyse the reshaping of social relations by globalization and digital technologies, a notion articulated by Xiang Biao, a prominent Chinese anthropologist and public intellectual. Modern individuals, according to Xiang, increasingly focus on the 'self' (personal aspirations) and the 'global' (abstract, distant issues) while neglecting the 'nearby': the immediate social spaces of neighbourhoods, communities and everyday interactions. This erosion of the 'nearby' leads to social fragmentation, atomized individuals and weakened collective agency. The concept of 'nearby' thus challenges binary frameworks like 'local vs global': Xiang uses it as a nuanced tool to dissect China's rapid urbanization, where traditional community ties have dissolved amid hypermobility and virtual connectivity. 'The nearby' (*fujin* in Chinese) is a lived space where one encounters people with diverse backgrounds on a regular basis. The nearby brings different positions into one view, thus constituting a 'scope' of seeing. Such a scope enables nuanced understandings of reality and facilitates new social relations and actions. The nearby could form a line of resistance against the power of the state, capital and technology, that is turning local communities into units of administrative control and value extraction.[14]

Xiang is well aware that this concept has universal scope – on the condition that we treat it as a concrete universality, specifying its scope with regard to each specific social context. Western societies have been witnessing for decades the gradual disintegration of 'the nearby'; in small towns, the open city square, once the centre of social interaction, has been replaced by the controlled space of shopping malls (when I visited Irvine south of LA many years ago, the city even boasted that there were no longer any public streets with shops and cafeterias there – a true nightmare of a place).

This tension between the similar-sounding notions of nearby and neighbour provides the key to the racist logic of Trumpian populism: populists try to enact the return of a nearby space – but it is a fake return. Its true territories are places like Elon Musk's Starbase town in Texas, a neo-feudal settlement controlled by a digital master. Instead of authentic local community we get the worst technocratic excesses: Bannon's noble fight against corporate power is the purest exercise of that same power.

The Ambivalence of De-commodification

Before 1990, Communist countries measured their ultimate progress by the quantity of steel produced. This obsession proved to be their downfall; the goal of China's Great Leap Forward in the late 1950s, which ended in a mega-catastrophe with tens of millions dead from starvation, was the direct result of a desire to surpass steel production in the UK. A possible parallel can be seen in our contemporary obsession with AI, which, in the years since ChatGPT's emergence, has been characterized by a preoccupation with scale. Companies have raced to build ever-larger models, train on datasets of unimaginable size, and spend billions on the infrastructure required to sustain this rapid growth.[1]

No wonder the launch of the new chatbot by China's DeepSeek was perceived as a wake-up call for US tech firms in the global race to dominate artificial intelligence. The emergence of DeepSeek, which has built its R1 model chatbot at a fraction of the cost of competitors, wiped $1tn in value from the leading US tech index on 27 January 2025, and although values were later largely recuperated, the effects of this shock lingered.[2] The launch of DeepSeek's R1 model was compared to a pivotal moment in the US–USSR Space Race: it was called AI's 'Sputnik moment' (referring to the Soviet Union 'beating' the US by launching the first satellite into orbit).

The predominant reactions of the American economic and political establishment were, as expected, full of hypocrisy. The same day, Trump commented on the ability of the DeepSeek chatbot to deliver the same performance as existing AI models with far fewer resources, threatening the dominance of the US-led AI boom: 'That's good because you don't have to spend as much money. I view that as a positive, as an asset.'[3] Trump's bluster barely concealed his awareness of how bad this development was for the US. Along the same lines, Sam Altman, the chief executive officer of OpenAI, said: 'DeepSeek's R1 is an impressive model, particularly around what they're able to deliver for the price. We will obviously deliver much better models and also it's legit invigorating to have a new competitor.'[4] One might argue that if it was *that* obvious that American firms would be able to effortlessly regain their superiority in the race for AI, the US wouldn't be in such a visible panic after falling behind.

There is also an ideological point to be made, which is rarely mentioned: the DeepSeek assistant and its underlying code is publicly accessible and can be downloaded for free, which is anathema to Trump's fundamental adherence to the most brutally free of free markets. Trump is aware of the importance of AI, but he approaches it in the old-fashioned 'bigger is better' Communist way: he announced a $500 billion investment, involving three top tech firms creating a new company called Stargate (even the name references a bygone pop-culture era) to grow AI infrastructure in the US. However, in 2023, Biden imposed a significant executive order which 'aimed to establish standards for the safe, secure and trustworthy development of AI across various sectors'.[5] On the first day of his second term in office, Trump revoked this order – a clear display of what his 'liberalism' effectively amounts to, that is, libertarianism unleashed: corporate neo-feudal masters freed to act without restraint and exempted from public control. Revoking this order signalled clearly that Trump does not think that the public needs or has a right to know the extent or nature of AI involvement in their lives. The public at large will be largely ignorant of the ways in which AI systems can control and regulate our lives.

As for the other side of the story, critics were quick to point out that DeepSeek censors itself in real time: it formulates its answers with a preamble of reasoning that it then erases before delivering its response to the user – as a journalist put it cynically, it works well until you ask it about Tiananmen Square and Taiwan.[6] Instead of feeling smug when we hear this, we should immediately ask the Socratic question: In what precise sense are we in the 'free West' any more free than the Chinese, really? There may be fewer topics which Western media is directly forbidden to mention, but that hardly equates to transparency; just think about the biased coverage from the big media outlets on the war in Gaza, not to mention how little we know about crises and conflicts which the media simply ignores. Moreover, the way our attention is manipulated when we browse through digital media is much more effective for a simple reason: we experience our scrolling and clicking as totally free and autonomously self-directed, but the most dangerous form of unfreedom is that which is experienced as freedom. Deepseek's blank silence when asked about Tiananmen Square at least makes us aware of the limits of our freedoms, while in the Western world of 'free', limitless media consumption, these limits are invisible and for that reason all the more effective.

The uncomfortable ambivalences raised by Deepseek's R1 model were teased out elegantly by Zorana Baković, who wrote that the release was a warning, alerting us to the need to think about China in a 'thoroughly new way': 'China has already proved that one can establish a free market without a free consumer, it has shown us that capitalism can thrive in the midst of communism – and did it not just now give us a warning that even a technological breakthrough can happen in a society without freedom of thinking?'[7] The implication of this ambivalence is the one spelled out by Yanis Varoufakis apropos the fall of the Assad regime in Syria:

> there is nothing confusing about condemning both Assad's regime and the US-backed jihadists that overthrew him. Not only is there no contradiction but it is the only right and effective way to be anti-imperialist. Not only is it not neutrality but it is the only right and effective way to take the side of the many, not the few.[8]

And the same applies to China. Yes, many things about Chinese politics and society (including the tightening censorship of intellectual and artistic life) should make us wary of placing too much trust in China as the main anti-imperialist power today. But the situation we are confronted with is not so much a Cold War-style clash of ideologies as a struggle between factions of global capital, and our duty is not to take sides in this conflict but to ruthlessly exploit and manipulate one competitor against the other. In the case of AI we should unconditionally support China against the commodification of AI on which the US relies, while remaining critical of China. The paradox is that, in the case of AI (which is *the* case in today's economy), China is on the side of small dynamic capitalist ventures against corporate neo-feudalism – in a nutshell, China is in this case both more authentically capitalist *and* more authentically socialist than the US.[9]

At a deeper level, however, we should not overestimate the impact of DeepSeek. As Varoufakis instantly observed,[10] DeepSeek will unsettle attempts to commodify digital programs, to sell them and make big profits in this way, but it will in no way disturb the smooth functioning of digital neo-feudalists like Jeff Bezos. Amazon provides us with the software which enables us to browse and buy on Amazon, for free – the catch is that this program not only collects data about ourselves and our desires and sells them on to other parties, it also imperceptibly regulates our 'free' choices of what to buy or watch.

The paradox is thus that the de-commodification of AI programs, although promising a move away from capitalism as we know it, ultimately only serves to strengthen the reign of our new feudal masters. To resolve this, one must leave behind the Marxist obsession with the commodification of everything, of all spheres of life, from politics to sexuality. One should not be afraid to give commodification its due: commodification means that I meet others in the market as a formally free individual and buy what I think I need. The solution is thus social control over digital clouds, their full transparency – in short, the solution is our control over *what we get for free*. This is not a plea for some kind of ethical capitalism, but a warning that what our new techno-feudal masters are giving us for free can be more enslaving than our dependence on market exchange.

Not to mention the fact that, in the complex pathology of human relations, money can also play a very positive role. Towards the end of Halina Reijn's 2024 film *Babygirl* (otherwise much overrated), there is a scene which deserves attention. Romy (Nicole Kidman), the CEO of a robotic process automation company, has engaged in a passionate BDSM love affair with the much younger Samuel who, although he is her subordinate, participates in rituals of domination and humiliation, allowing her to realize her submissive fantasies. In the final scene, Romy and Jacob, her husband, are at home, having rekindled their relationship – they re-enact the type of rough sex that Romy was introduced to by Samuel, although she is only able to orgasm by imagining Samuel playing with the dog in the hotel room that they shared earlier in the film (a clear case of the split between the actual sexual act and its fantasy support which is present in all our sex lives). Just before this final scene, Romy is visited by an elder board member in her office, who informs her that Samuel has taken a new job in Japan. He asks if she had anything to do with Samuel leaving, seemingly implying he knows about the affair, and invites her to his house when he is alone – in short, he expresses his readiness to play the same masochist games with her. Disgusted, Romy firmly states that she is unafraid of him and tells him to leave her office, and the precise words she uses are crucial: 'If I want to be humiliated, I'm going to pay someone to do it.' Money allows Romy to retain her dignity while allowing her partner to humiliate her: it allows her to act as the master of her own humiliation.

Decolonization and the Public Use of Reason

What is going on in the world in November 2025? Zohran Mamdani's victory in New York is the bright exception to the predominant drift towards more and more of the usual. In the Middle East, we get the usual mix of violence and obscenity. Major General Yifat Tomer-Yerushalmi, who less than a week ago was 'the Israeli military's top lawyer, tasked with enforcing the rule of law within the nation's armed forces', is now under arrest as part of a criminal investigation into the leak of a video showing the alleged abuse, including sexual abuse, of Palestinian detainees in a notorious Israeli military prison. In her resignation letter, Tomer-Yerushalmi wrote:

> There are things that cannot be done even against the worst of the detainees. Officers of the [legal] unit have faced repeated personal attacks, harsh insults, and even real threats. All of this because they stood guard over the rule of law in the IDF – together with the commanders and alongside them.[1]

The last traces of dignity have been erased from public life in Israel, a country in which Itamar Bin Gvir, the minister who controls security in the West Bank, is a racist criminal convicted by an Israeli court. Today, his shadow hovers above the terror to which West Bank Palestinians are exposed on a daily basis. CNN reported that the olive harvest in the occupied West Bank, once 'a time of history, culture and tradition', has been transformed into 'a season of fear' with more than 200 attacks by settlers in the past month, according to the Palestinian Authority. The Israeli military told CNN it 'recognizes the importance of the olive harvest in maintaining the fabric of life in the region', but acknowledged it has restricted entry to certain areas in order to 'prevent friction'.[2] I agree in principle, but what about restricting the entry of settlers to Palestinian fields with olives?

But this should not blind us to other horrors taking place around the world. Just recall how traffickers deep in the Sahara are extorting ransom payments from refugees' families. In southern Libya there are camps where hundreds of migrants on their way from Sudan or Eritrea to the Libyan coast are kept prisoners and mercilessly tortured (tied up, urinated on, kicked, and beaten with a metal pole). Videos of these tortures are then sent to their relatives, with the message that the prisoners will be tortured to death if the relatives don't pay money for their release.[3]

Perhaps the ultimate case of these horrors are the scam factories at the triangle of the Thai, Laos and Myanmar borders.[4] Western media recently reported on the fate of Vera Kravtsova, a twenty-six-year-old model from Minsk, who was allegedly killed and sold for organs in Myanmar.[5] Vera recently came across an advert offering part-time modelling work in Thailand. She flew to Bangkok, where she found herself in labour slavery. On 20 September, she was taken to the city of Yangon in Myanmar where she had to work in a scam centre, a place where girls flirt with men on dating sites, enticing them to invest in something and then transferring the funds to scammers. When she was no longer able to fulfil her quota, she was allegedly moved to another building where her organs were sold to people in foreign countries needing them, and then she was killed. To add insult to injury, the scam company demanded $500,000 from her relatives for her body, and a few days later they said that the deceased was cremated. Now the family is negotiating the return of ashes to their homeland.

It is typical that this case was widely reported because it concerned a white girl kidnapped by evil 'Oriental' monsters. But the scam centres of Myanmar, particularly along the Thai border, are a gigantic organization: they turn around more money than any state in the world after the US and China, plus the majority of their 'slaves' are from Asian countries. According to reporting by Western newspapers, these scam centres expanded after the 2021 military coup in Myanmar, with compounds such as KK Park 'operating as heavily fortified hubs for transnational online fraud':

Facilities include luxury housing for managers, on-site hospitals, banks and internet access via satellites like Starlink, enabling operations despite Thai border restrictions.... Controlled by crime syndicates and tacitly supported by the military, these complexes use trafficked workers from across Asia and Africa, forcing them to run scams under threats of torture and violence ...[6]

By October 2025, around 7,000 people had been released from scam centres run by criminal gangs and warlords, but this number is just a fraction of an estimated 100,000 people trapped along the border.[7] Crime groups are reportedly using AI to write scamming scripts, exploiting increasingly realistic deepfake technology to create personae, pose as people seeking romantic opportunities and mask their identity, voice and gender. The crime syndicates have quickly adopted cryptocurrency and are investing in cutting-edge technological developments to move money more quickly, as well as making the scams more effective.[8]

Although the US administration would undoubtedly publicly condemn such events, its global politics is creating a world in which such acts are silently tolerated as long as they are not perceived as a threat by some big power. For example, China only put pressure on Myanmar when it discovered that these gangs also scammed many Chinese citizens. The ultimate cruel irony resides in the fact that, since these scam centres are organized by Asian criminal lords, and since their targets are mostly individuals from Western countries (as well as the Chinese new upper classes), they like to present their activity as a form of struggle against colonialism: they claim that they are just taking back from the colonizers a part of what the colonizers took from their in the past. We should absolutely not dismiss this claim as a cynical lie but consider it an extreme consequence of what is wrong with the discourse of so-called decolonization.

Benjamin Zachariah's *The Postcolonial Volk*[9] deals with this dark side of decolonization in an exemplary way. When I first picked it up, the first two paragraphs of the preface to the book grabbed me so thoroughly that I instantly knew a sleepless night was ahead of me. Zachariah begins with the assertion that postcolonial theory and its bedfellow, decolonial theory, are the most flourishing products of academia in recent times. Transcending their origins in universities and literary criticism, and clustering around what is coming to be known as 'theory from the Global South', their guiding assumptions have leaked into the public domain and become shibboleths with which to acknowledge historically victimised communities. With this success has come a disturbing trend: political activity operates based on clumsy victimhood analogies, and much of its rhetoric is deliberately anti-rational, reproducing and perpetuating the manufactured categories of racist and sectarian imaginations.

Zachariah focuses on the worrying affinities of postcolonial thought with *völkisch* thinking. *Völkisch* is a German adjective that indicates a community of blood, soil and race (that's why the Nazis spoke about *Volksgemeinschaft*). Postcolonialists, of course, don't put things in this direct way; they instead invoke a community of collective memory and victimhood. Nonetheless, Zachariah argues, that older form of collective belonging remains embedded in apparently new attitudes: a compulsory community of both inherited victimhood and organic belonging, unity of collective memory and victimhood. Zachariah condenses the postcolonial theory in what he ironically calls the 'twelve iron rules of history', the first of which holds that the only universal right is the right to be offended. And the eighth rule: the age of reason is the age of empire – which is why postcolonialists claim to have relegated Marx to the dustbin of history, while reconceptualizing class struggle and exploitation as cultural struggle of ethnic identities. One should not shirk from calling this stance by its proper name: it is Fascism in a new guise.

So how can we in the West deal with our colonial legacy without falling into the trap of postcolonialism and decolonization? The now half-forgotten opening ceremony of the 2024 Paris Olympics shows the way. What does this ceremony and the Marvel superhero blockbuster *Deadpool & Wolverine* have in common? Both offer a dazzling spectacle saturated with irony – but that is about all the latter offers, so this superficial resemblance should not make us blind to their profound incompatibility. Comparing the two offers a clear insight into the profoundly ambiguous nature of irony today.

Irony, ironic distance towards the social order and its values, can function a mode of perfect conformism – if this sounds incredible, go and see Shawn Levy's 2024 film, the latest in the series based on Marvel comics, which was quite aptly characterized by Wendy Ide as proof that a movie 'can be obnoxious and simultaneously very funny. But it's also slapdash, repetitive and shoddy looking, with an overreliance on meme-derived gags and achingly meta comic fan in-jokes.'[10] This is precisely how ideology functions today: it fills up the void left by its central message, which is no longer taken seriously by anyone, with self-referential jokes, multiverse-hopping and directly addressing the public. This is how we are able to endure the single crazy violent world we live in. Just recall how Trump's brutally authoritarian measures are accompanied not only by vulgar sexist and racist remarks but also tasteless self-referential jokes.

But there is also a different mode of irony, one masterfully practised by Thomas Jolly, the curator of the Paris 2024 Summer Olympics opening ceremony. He was widely criticized although he closely followed the Olympic Charter which mandates that the proceedings should include 'an artistic program showcasing the culture of the host country and city, the parade of athletes and the lighting of the Olympic cauldron'.[11] So what provoked these negative reactions? If we ignore simple confusion (some Catholics condemned the spectacle for staging the Last Supper as a transvestite orgy, but in this scene Jolly's reference was a well-known image of Bacchanalian festivities, not da Vinci's *Last Supper*), the gist of the criticism was best articulated by the Hungarian Prime Minister, Viktor Orban:

> Westerners believe that nation states no longer exist. They deny that there is a common culture and a public morality based on it. There is no morality and if you watched the opening of the Olympic Games yesterday, you will have seen it.[12]

For Orban, the ceremony was a sign of Europe's spiritual suicide, while for Jolly (and many of us, I hope), the ceremony was one of the rare manifestations of an authentically European legacy. France is the country of Descartes, the founder of modern philosophy, and Descartes' starting point of radical universal doubt is grounded in, precisely, a 'multicultural' experience of how one's own tradition is no better than what appears to us as the 'eccentric' traditions of others:

> I had been taught, even in my College days, that there is nothing imaginable so strange or so little credible that it has not been maintained by one philosopher or other, and I further recognized in the course of my travels that all those whose sentiments are very contrary to ours are yet not necessarily barbarians or savages, but may be possessed of reason in as great or even a greater degree than ourselves.[13]

Only through such relativization of particular ethnic roots can we arrive at an authentic universalist position. In Kantian terms, when we reflect upon our ethnic roots, we engage in a *private use of reason*, constrained by contingent dogmatic presuppositions. In other words, we act as 'immature' individuals, not as free human beings who dwell in the dimension of the universality of reason. This is why, in a famous passage of his essay 'What is Enlightenment?', Immanuel Kant opposes such private use of reason to the public use of reason, its use in the public space of the 'world-civil-society'. For Kant, what is 'private' is not defined by the opposition between the individual and communal ties; 'private' is the very communal-institutional order of one's particular identification: the state and its laws, religion and its institutions are private, while 'public' is the transnational universality of the exercise of one's reason. We saw this in action in the Paris Olympics ceremony: a rare glimmer of the emancipatory potential of Europe. Yes, France and Paris, but not limited to the 'private use of reason': France and Paris made fun of themselves, but in a thoroughly benevolent way, the irony and jokes maintaining a distance towards every 'private' institutional frame, including that of the French state.

Conservatives were, of course, wrong when they claimed that the ceremony was a display of LGBT ideology and of politically correct uniformity. The ceremony was directed against conservative nationalism; however, in its content and in its style, it was directed even more against stiff, reductive 'politically correct' moralism. Instead of worrying about diversity and inclusion in the standard PC mode (where all who do not agree with our notion of inclusion are excluded), the show just let all races and sexes dance. Marie

Antoinette's guillotined head singing, the Mona Lisa painting which floated in the Seine, the joyful Bacchanalia with half-naked bodies... Is such an ironic and obscene spectacle not the opposite of political correctness? Numerous other details point in the same direction – workers repairing Notre Dame were seen dancing at their workplace; the show did not take place at a stadium, the entire city opened itself up to it, with events on the river and in the historical buildings along the Seine.[14] The ceremony presented Europe at its best – only in Europe is such a ceremony possible. The ceremony was ironic, staged at a distance from one's own tradition, but precisely as such it displayed fidelity to the emancipatory aspects of this tradition. It was messy, including inconsistent moments, but the message was delivered from the standpoint of France, or of Paris even, the greatest city in the world. This is why Žiga Turk, a Slovene conservative nationalist, was deeply wrong when he wrote apropos my celebration of the Paris Olympics opening ceremony as an emancipatory act:

> Emancipation is euphemism for uprootedness. The ceremony was a feast of uprooting Europe from its humus. Some people celebrate this, others deplore it.[15]

On the contrary, the very form of the ceremony was deeply rooted in French culture. Turk's reproach is one of profound conservativism; it discreetly relies on the old German opposition between culture and civilization which was elaborated in detail by Thomas Mann in his *Reflections of a Nonpolitical Man* (first published in German in 1918)[16] where he defends the authoritarianism and 'culture' of Germany against the 'civilization' of the West, especially Great Britain and France. Its central motif is the dichotomy between 'civilization' and 'culture': civilization, according to Thomas Mann, 'involves reason, enlightenment, moderation, moral education, skepticism'; culture represents the opposite, 'the sublimation of the demonic' – discipline and dedication, war, against democracy and pragmatism.[17]

Crucially, Mann characterizes himself as 'apolitical', dismissing politics and praising the total dedication to a cause which is at work in art, warfare and other forms of total engagement. Mann is well aware that there is a deadly 'demonic' dimension to such total dedication which, in Freud's terms, reaches 'beyond the pleasure principle' – it is the domain of death-drive. What art achieves is the 'sublimation of the demonic', i.e., the elevation of the self-destructive death-drive into a form of culture – are all Wagner's operas not about a culture of dying, about how to find fulfilment in death? When Freud speaks about '*Unbehagen in der Kultur*', the uneasiness of our dwelling in culture, he isn't talking only about the fact that cultural norms and demands oppress our instincts; what he really takes aim at is the deadly, self-destructive dimension of culture itself which threatens to seduce us into the excessive *jouissance* of its crazy rituals. This is why we need not only realist pragmatism embodied in the English-speaking world but also civilization in the specific French sense of good manners and playfulness – civilization makes culture more bearable.

The dichotomy Mann constructs between culture and civilization (which recurs at a slightly different level in his later novel *The Magic Mountain*) is a false one: there is no place in it for a radical Left stance, one which underpinned the Paris Olympics ceremony. A world in which the Olympic opening ceremony of Paris 2024 is best characterized by the remarks of Aleksandr Dugin on his podcast with Pepe Escobar.[18] For Dugin, Europe is now irrelevant, a relic of history, a rotten garden protected by a high wall, and the only choice is the one between the American globalist deep state and a peaceful new world order of sovereign states respecting each other's right to exist. (How do we know this world will be peaceful? Because, according to Dugin, Russia will distribute nuclear arms to all Third World states, so that every conflict will lead to mutual destruction – nobody in the West will risk war and the world will be at peace ...). That's why, for Dugin, the 2024 American presidential elections decided the fate of humanity on earth: the choice was between the US deep state and Trump. Since Trump won, de-escalation is now possible; had Kamala Harris won, a global war and the end of humanity would have awaited us – in short, Trump is a rational pragmatic businessman who 'has no mission but the one of the salvation of humanity'.[19] True, but the kind of peace Trump is bringing can be clearly seen apropos of Gaza and Ukraine: an enforced peace which ignores the victims since it is based on the negotiation between the superpowers

There are two further stupid reproaches to the Paris ceremony that are easy to reject. Firstly, it is easy to make fun of our Christian tradition, but why didn't Jolly also make fun of Islam, of Buddhism ...? Secondly, isn't it falsely naive to celebrate joyful peace while our world is at war and full of catastrophes? Making fun of our own tradition is a prerogative of the West, the resource of our strength, and a challenge to others: why are you afraid to do it? A joyful celebration of peaceful diversity is in itself a critique of our sad reality. Against what people like Orban and Dugin might think, the message of the ceremony was deeply ethical. It tells conservative nationalists: watch the ceremony carefully again and be ashamed of what you are!

Let It Rot . . .

Something important is going on in China, a massive tendency among the young which has engendered panic in leadership circles: the spirit of passive resignation rendered by a new buzzword, '*bai lan*' ('let it rot'). Born of economic disillusionment and pushback against long-standing cultural norms, *bai lan* advocates a minimalistic approach to work: working only the minimum required hours, and prioritizing personal well-being over career advancement. The same tendency is also encapsulated by '*Tang ping*' ('lying flat'), a slang neologism that stands for choosing to 'lie down flat and get over the beatings' via a low-desire, more indifferent attitude towards life. Both terms signal a personal rejection of societal pressures to overwork and over-achieve, dismissing social engagement as a rat race with ever diminishing returns.

This tendency is not limited to the younger generation – consider another phenomenon: in July 2024, the media reported on a growing number of Chinese workers swapping high-pressure office jobs for flexible blue-collar work. Li, 27, from Wuhan said:

> I like cleaning up. As living standards improve (across the country), the demand for housekeeping services is also surging with an ever-expanding market. The change it brings is that my head no longer feels dizzy. I feel less mental pressure. And I am full of energy every day.[1]

Such a stance presents itself as apolitical: it rejects both violent resistance to the institutions of power and dialogue with those in power. Are there other options? The mass protests in Serbia are even more important than *bai lan* in China: they are unique because they do offer a third option. They are the true opposite of *bai lan*: protestors admit that there is something rotten in the state of Serbia, but they do care about it (or rather, they still have the hope of being able to do something about it), they are not ready to just let it rot.

The protests began in November 2024 in Novi Sad following the collapse of the canopy of the city's railway station, which left fifteen people dead and two severely injured.[2] At the time of writing, protests have spread to 200 cities and towns in Serbia and are ongoing. Although they are led by university students who demand accountability for the canopy collapse, hundreds of thousands have participated in many of them – the biggest student-led movement in Europe since 1968. Obviously, the canopy collapse was a kind of catalyst for this volcanic explosion: a point at which the dissatisfaction which had become more and more widespread in Serbia finally detonated. The protesters' concerns are not only about corruption and ecology (like the plan of the government to activate big lithium mines); they also rebuff the way the Serbian president Aleksandar Vučić and his government are treating the population. What is presented by the government as a fast-track route to modernization and inclusion into the global market covers up a thick web of corruption, a sell-out of national resources to foreign investors under shady conditions, a gradual elimination of opposition media, up to the suspicious deaths of visible opponents of the regime (often masked as traffic accidents) – all this is happening in a blatant way which displays the government's obscene rejection of basic decency. The situation is now much worse than in the worst years of Milošević's regime. But, again, what makes these protests unique?

Protesters repeat again and again: 'We have no political demands and keep our distance from opposition parties. We simply ask that Serbian institutions work in the interest of citizens.'[3] They have formulated only a couple of demands on which they unconditionally insist: the publication of all documentation on the renovation of the Novi Sad train station, with full access to ensure that the government is not hiding anything from the public; the dropping of charges against those who were arrested during the first anti-government protest in November; criminal charges to be brought against those who attacked students during the protests in Belgrade (some people, who later turned out to be members of the ruling party, physically attacked protesters). In short, the protesters want to break the vicious circle of a state held hostage by a ruling party that controls all institutions.

Vučić's reaction is not just violence in many different forms but also a version of what in boxing is called clinching: a technique in which one boxer leans on an opponent and wraps their arms to prevent them from punching freely. The more panic-stricken Vučić becomes, the more fervently he invites the protesters to engage in a dialogue, to negotiate (as it is done in civilized countries, he likes to add). However, the protesters refuse any dialogue, they just insist on their demands. Protests usually rely on at least a threat of violence while at the same time they express their readiness for a truly open dialogue in which they will be taken seriously by the ruling regime. Here the situation is the opposite: there is no threat of violence, but there is also a clear rejection of any dialogue. This insistence on demands causes confusion in its very simplicity, giving birth to conspiracy theories: who is behind it all? The fact that no leading figures are emerging in the protests adds to the (false appearance of) confusion. (The reason for this is also that any leading figure could be the target of the regime's counter-measures.)

Protests in Serbia are thus, in some sense, similar to *bai lan* in China: the standard political engagement, dissidence included, is absent. At some point, of course, organized politics will have to enter the game, but the protesters' 'apolitical' stance aims to ensure that the new politics will not just be a version of the old game – the table has to be cleared for an authentic state of law and order to be realized. This is why one should support the protests unconditionally: they prove that in some situations, a simple call for law and order can be more subversive than anarchic violence. Protesters want law and order without the set of unwritten rules that spin it towards corruption and authoritarian power. Protesters are thus far from the old anarchic Left that dominated the 1968 student protests. After the Serbian students blocked a bridge over the River Danube in Novi Sad for 24 hours, they decided to extend their protest for three additional hours while they cleaned up the area where they had been holding their rally. Can one even imagine the Paris students throwing stones at police afterwards cleaning the streets of the Latin Quarter of (their own) rubble?

However, whatever the protesters' intentions, their protest is deeply political – so are they in some sense hypocritical? No, they are not, precisely because they are political in a much more radical way: they don't want to play politics within the existing space of (mostly unwritten) rules, they want to change the basic way state institutions work in Serbia. The truly hypocritical agent in this affair sits in Brussels. It is the European Union, which puts no pressure on Vučić because of the fear that he will turn to Russia. While the EU Commission President Ursula von der Leyen expressed support for 'the Georgian people fighting for democracy', she has remained remarkably quiet about the uprising in Serbia – a country that has officially been a candidate for EU membership since 2012.[4] The EU has so far let Aleksandar Vučić have his way because, as some commentators have noted, he promises stability and lithium.[5] This lack of criticism from the EU, even in the face of massive electoral fraud, has repeatedly left Serbian civil society out in the cold. This is why Serb protests are not another colour revolution, not another 'join the democratic West' movement, and there are no EU flags carried by protesters. As far as the protesters are concerned, when it comes to the EU, their attitude is *bai lan*: let it rot, it's not even worth getting involved. In short, after the seeming nadir of the war in Gaza, the EU has reached another ethico-political low.

We live in the midst of a dark period in which even the words our big media use to describe the ongoing horrors mystify the situation in a ridiculous way. In summer 2025, the US accepted fifty-nine Boers from South Africa, deploying the official justification that they were escaping a genocide of Boers.[6] Meanwhile, the actual full-scale genocide in Gaza qualifies as Israel's self-defence.

In a time of such bleakness, signs of hope are more precious than ever. One such event was the unanimous decision of the PKK (Kurdistan Workers' Party) on 12 May 2025 to follow the advice of its leader Abdullah Ocalan (imprisoned for over two decades) and engage in the total dissolution of the organization.[7] The PKK is a militant political organization and armed guerrilla group primarily based in the mountainous Kurdish-majority regions of southeastern Turkey, northern Iraq and north-eastern Syria. It was founded in 1978 and was involved in asymmetric warfare in the Kurdish–Turkish conflict (with several ceasefires between 1993 and 2013–15). Although the PKK initially sought an independent Kurdish state, in the 1990s its official platform changed to seeking autonomy and increased political and cultural rights for Kurds within Turkey. Over the past few decades, not only has the PKK moved closer to a peaceful solution but Ocalan himself, studying in prison, has also engaged in deep reflections on issues like feminism and philosophical issues. In short, PKK became a movement which was fully part of the modern Left.

The effects of this reorientation were also felt among Kurds living outside Turkey. What happened in Iran in 2022 – the so-called Mahsa Amini protests – had a world-historical significance. The protests, which spread to dozens of cities, began in Tehran on 16 September 2022, as a reaction to the death of Amini, a 22-year-old woman of Kurdish origins who died in police custody. She was beaten to death by the Guidance Patrol, known as the Islamic 'morality police', after being arrested for wearing an 'improper' hijab. The protests combined different struggles (against women's oppression, against religious oppression, for political freedom against state terror) into an organic unison. Iran is culturally different from the 'developed West', so Zan, Zendegi, Azadi ('Woman, Life, Freedom', the slogan of the protests) is very different from the 'Me Too' movement in Western countries. Iran's protests mobilized millions of ordinary women, and was directly linked to the struggle of all, men included – there is no apparent anti-male tendency, as can be the case with Western feminism. Women and men acted together against the common enemy of religious fundamentalism supported by state terror. Men who participated in Zan, Zendegi, Azadi knew that the struggle for women's rights was also the struggle for their own freedom. The non-Kurd protesters also saw that the oppression of Kurds limited their own freedom – solidarity with Kurds is the only way towards freedom in Iran. Iranian protests thus realized what Western Leftists can only dream about. They avoided some of the traps of Western middle-class feminism by recognizing that the struggle for women's freedom is also the struggle of all people against ethnic oppression, against religious fundamentalism, and against state terror.

So what about the reproach that the PKK nonetheless began as an agent of violent struggle? The PKK just followed the general rule of resistance: if one is to be taken seriously, one has to begin with the threat of violent resistance. When a peaceful negotiation wins over armed resistance, armed resistance is inscribed in the result. We tend to celebrate two successful negotiations – the rise of the ANC to power in South Africa and the peaceful protests led by Martin Luther King in the US. However, in both cases it is obvious that the (relative) victory of the peaceful negotiations occurred because the establishment feared violent resistance (from the more radical wing of ANC as well as from black Americans). In short, negotiations succeeded because they were accompanied by a superposed ominous threat of armed struggle.

The surprise might be that this is happening in Kurdistan, a place still generally viewed by Western eyes as a place of brutal tribal warfare, naive honesty and a sense of honour, but also of superstition, betrayal and permanent cruel warfare – the almost caricatural barbaric Other of European 'civilization'. If we look at contemporary Kurds, we cannot but be surprised by the contrast to this cliché – in Turkey, where I know the situation relatively well, I noticed that the Kurdish minority is the most modern and secular part of society, at a distance from every religious fundamentalism, with developed feminism, etc. (Let me just mention a detail that I learned in Istanbul: restaurants owned by Kurds have no tolerance for any sign of superstition ...) In his first term, Trump tried to justify his betrayal of Kurds (he condoned the Turkish attack on the Kurdish enclave in northern Syria) by noting that 'Kurds are no angels'.[8] Naturally not, since, for him, the only angels in that region are Israel (especially on the West Bank) and Saudi Arabia (especially in Yemen). And yet, in some sense, they are the only angels in that part of the world.

The fate of the Kurds makes them the exemplary victim of geopolitical colonial games: spread along the borderline of four neighbouring states (Turkey, Syria, Iraq, Iran), their (more than deserved) full autonomy was in nobody's interest, and they paid the full price for it. Do we still remember Saddam's mass bombing and gas-poisoning of Kurds in the north of Iraq in the early 1990s? More recently, when ISIS dominated large parts of Syria and Iraq, Turkey played a well-planned military-political game, officially fighting ISIS but effectively bombing Kurds who were really fighting

ISIS. And it should come as no surprise that a strong part of the Kurdish forces – Peshmerga, 'to stand in front of death' – were composed of women who achieved a legendary status as snipers.[9]

In the past few decades, the ability of the Kurds to organize their communal life was tested in almost clear-cut experimental conditions: the moment they were given a space to breath freely outside the conflicts of the states around them, they surprised the world. After Saddam's fall, the Kurdish enclave in northern Iraq developed into the only safe part of the country with well-functioning institutions and regular flights to Europe. In northern Syria, the Kurdish enclave centered in Rojava was a unique place in today's geopolitical mess: when Kurds were given a respite from their big neighbours who otherwise threatened them all the time, they quickly built a society that one cannot but designate an actually-existing and well-functioning utopia. From my own professional interest, I noticed the thriving intellectual community in Rojava where they repeatedly invited me to give lectures – these plans were brutally interrupted by the military tensions in the area.

But what especially saddened me was the reaction of some of my 'Leftist' colleagues who were bothered by the fact that Kurds also had to rely on American military protection – what should they have done, caught in the tensions between Turkey, the Syrian civil war, the Iraqi mess and Iran? Did they have any other choice? Should they sacrifice themselves on the altar of anti-imperialist solidarity?

That is why it is our duty to fully support the resistance of the Kurds and to rigorously denounce the dirty games Western powers play with them. While the sovereign states around them are gradually sinking into a new barbarism, Kurds are the only glimmer of hope. This struggle is not just fought by Kurds for Kurds, but is also about what kind of global new order is emerging. If Kurds are abandoned, we capitulate to a new order in which there will be no place for the most precious part of the European legacy of emancipation. If Europe turns away from Kurds, it will betray itself. The Europe which betrays Kurds will be the true Europastan!

One should thus conclude that Abdullah Ocalan is nothing less than a Kurdish Nelson Mandela: his proposal that the PKK should dissolve itself is an authentic courageous act of engaging oneself in the struggle for peace. Alongside him, one should mention Marwan Barghouti, the Palestinian Mandela who also sat in an Israeli prison for two decades. What will come out of the self-dissolution of the PKK depends on the Turkish government – will it embrace the offer with a sincere counter-gesture? Strong international pressure on Turkey is here urgently needed, and it is a duty of all of us to engage in it.

Re-staging the Event

Recall the staged performance of 'Storming the Winter Palace' in Petrograd, on the third anniversary of the October Revolution, on 7 November 1920.[1] Tens of thousands of workers, soldiers, students and artists worked round the clock, living on *kasha* (tasteless wheat porridge), tea and frozen apples, to prepare the performance at the very place where the event 'really took place' three years earlier. Their work was coordinated by army officers, as well as by avant-garde artists, musicians and directors, from Malevich to Meyerhold. Although this was acting and not 'reality', the soldiers and sailors were playing themselves – many of them had not only participated in the events of 1917, but were also simultaneously involved in the real battles of the Civil War that were raging in the near vicinity of Petrograd, a city under siege and suffering from severe shortages of food. A contemporary commented on the performance:

> 'The future historian will record how, throughout one of the bloodiest and most brutal revolutions, all of Russia was acting';[2] and the formalist theoretician Viktor Shklovsky noted that 'some kind of elemental process is taking place where the living fabric of life is being transformed into the theatrical'.[3]

But in the spirit of Socrates, we should submit this idea of 'living fabric transformed into the theatrical' to a closer critical analysis: what exactly was staged in 1920? Theatrical repetitions are never an innocent affair, they always subtly transform the reality they re-stage, especially if it is a reality as politically charged as that of the October Revolution:

> This reenactment, watched by 100,000 spectators, provided the model for official films made later, which showed fierce fighting

during the storming of the Winter Palace, although, in reality, the Bolshevik insurgents had faced little opposition.[4]

The Provisional Government had dwindled to a meeting of ministers in the Winter Palace. A few Red Guards climbed in through the servants' entrance and arrested them. (Prior to this attack, Kerensky himself escaped the Palace by simply driving off in his car.) One sailor was killed when his rifle went off in his hand; four Red Guards and one sailor were killed by stray bullets. That was the total death toll on this historic day: 'Most people in Petrograd weren't even aware that a revolution was taking place.'[5] In further anti-climactic style, Lenin had taken a streetcar the previous day to a Bolshevik meeting in order to declare a revolution, and almost got lost (although streetcars functioned very efficiently at the time). One can imagine him telling the driver: 'Sorry, I am in a hurry, I have to announce a revolution' ... A streetcar named revolution.

But it wasn't only this chaos that had to be erased from the official narrative. When the popular dissatisfaction in Russia grew and Lenin's revolutionary ideas gained momentum, the majority of the Bolshevik party leaders were already trying to organize a mass popular uprising. Trotsky advocated a view which, to traditional Marxists, couldn't but appear 'Blanquists': namely that a narrow, well-trained elite should take power. After a short oscillation, Lenin defended Trotsky.[6] Against the latter 'Trotskyite' defenders of an (almost) 'democratic' Trotsky who advocated authentic mass mobilization and grass-roots democracy, one should emphasize that Trotsky was all too well aware of the inertia of the 'masses' – he believed that the most one could expect of them was chaotic dissatisfaction. Hence his conviction that a small, well-trained revolutionary force should use this chaos to strike at power and thereby open up the space where the masses could organize themselves properly. Here, however, the crucial question arises: what would this elite force actually do? In what sense would it 'take power'? The true novelty of Trotsky becomes visible here: this force does not 'take power' in the traditional sense of a palace *coup d'état*, occupying government offices and army headquarters, etc.; it does not focus on confronting police or the army on the barricades. Let us quote some passages from Curzio Malaparte's unique *Coup d'Etat: The Technique of Revolution* (1932) to get the taste of it:

> Kerensky's police and the military authorities were especially concerned with the defense of the State's official and political organizations: the Government offices, the Maria Palace where the Republican council sat, the Tauride Palace, seat of the Duma, the Winter Palace, and General Headquarters. When Trotsky discovered this mistake he decided to attack only the technical branches of the national and municipal Government. Insurrection for him was only a question of technique. 'In order to overthrow the modern State,' he said, 'you need a storming party, technical experts and gangs of armed men led by engineers.'
>
> On the eve of the *coup d'état*, Trotsky told [Dzerzhinsky] that the Red Guards should leave Kerensky's government alone; that the important thing was to capture the State and not to fight the Government with machine-guns; that the Republican Council, the Ministries and the Duma played an unimportant part in the tactics of insurrection and should not be the objectives of an armed rebellion; that the key to the State lay, not in its political and secretarial organizations nor yet in the Tauride, Maria or Winter Palaces, but in its technical services, such as the electric stations, the telephone and telegraph offices, the port, gasworks and water mains.[7]

Trotsky thus targeted the material (technical) grid of power (railways, electricity, water supply, post, etc.), the mechanisms without which state power becomes utterly inoperative. According to legend, the morning after all this took place Trotsky said: 'OK, the revolution has been achieved, I am tired and I'll catch some sleep now!' Lenin and others went on to lead the mobilized masses to fight the police and storm the Winter Palace (performative acts without any real purpose or relevance) ...

Instead of indulging in a miserable moralist-democratic rejection of such a procedure, one should rather analyse it coldly and think about how to apply its lessons to today. It could be argued that Trotsky's strategies have gained new relevance with the progressive digitalization of our lives in what could be characterized as the new era of post-human power. Most of our activities (and passivities) are now registered in some digital cloud which also permanently evaluates us, tracing not only our acts but also our emotional states; when we experience ourselves as most free (surfing the internet where everything is available), we are totally 'externalized' and subtly manipulated. Everything is regulated by some digital network, from transport to health, from electricity to water. That's why the internet is our most important commons, the struggle for its control *the* struggle today. The enemy is the combination of privatized and state-controlled commons, corporations (Google, Facebook) and state security agencies (NSA).

The digital network that sustains the functioning of our societies as well as their control mechanisms is the ultimate figure of the technical grid that sustains power. Trotsky's idea that the power of the state lies not in its political and secretarial organizations but in its technical services and infrastructure appears extremely apposite. Consequently, in the same way that, for Trotsky, taking control of the post, electricity, railways, etc. was the key moment in the revolutionary seizing of power, is it not the case that today, the 'occupation' of the digital grid is absolutely crucial if we are to break the power of the state and capital? And, in the same way as Trotsky required the mobilization of an elite well-trained 'storming party [made up of] technical experts and gangs of armed men led by engineers' to resolve this 'question of technique', the lesson of the past few decades is that neither massive grass-roots protest nor well-organized political movements with elaborated political visions are enough. We also need a narrow strike force of dedicated 'engineers' (hackers, whistle-blowers ...), organized as a disciplined conspiratorial group. Its task will be to 'take over' the digital grid, to rip it forcefully out of the hands of corporations and state agencies which now de facto control it.

This brings us back to our starting point: an event is re-staged as a theatrical performance in order to obfuscate the reality of this event, in order to make it fit the ideological image of this event, or – more precisely – in order to *construct* this image. Through its re-staging, the October Revolution retroactively becomes what it should have been as the founding event of a new socio-political order. There is a strange parallel between this restaging and the status of justice – recall the well-known aphorism: 'Justice must not only be done, but must also be seen to be done.' This dictum was laid down by Lord Hewart, then Lord Chief Justice of England, in 1924. He went on to observe that what was important was not what was actually done, but what might appear to have been done, and held: 'Nothing is to be done which creates even a suspicion that there has been an improper interference with the course of justice.'[8] The motif for re-staging the October Revolution was homologous: 'Nothing is to be done which creates even a suspicion that there has been an improper interference with the proper course of the revolution.' The purity of the (retroactively established) narrative has to be protected even if the most important factor in the true narrative – Trotsky's blueprint for undermining a state – is lost in the process.

All past revolutions reshaped their image even without a literal re-staging: in the case of the French Revolution, the fall of the Bastille, a ridiculously unimportant event in which seven not-very-notable prisoners were freed, was afterwards elevated into one of the founding images of the revolution. Today, however, something new and weird is gradually emerging: when those in power enact a horrifying crime, they no longer even pretend to obfuscate it through a re-staging (or re-interpretation) that presents it as a noble act. In Gaza and on the West Bank, in Ukraine, etc., crimes are boastfully presented as what they are, in all their enormity and obscenity. The media was right to call the destruction of Gaza the first TV-transmitted genocide. The slogan 'justice not only has to be done, it has to be done in a visible way' is thus reversed: evil (ethnic cleansing, genocidal violence ...) not only has to be done, it should appear as what it is, as pure evil no longer masked by some honest cause.

How are we to fight this fully cynical obscenity which seems to preclude any affective critique since, in their perverse honesty, the perpetrators admit (even trumpet) in advance the dirty details our critical analysis brings out? There is a gap that persists in this obscenity. The state powers do not just simply identify with the evil they commit: in their public declarations, they still talk about peace, humanity (the IDF continues to claim to be the most humane army in the world, etc.). In short, the two levels coexist: the state continues to talk dispassionately about peace and humanity, without any subjective commitment behind it, while in public opinion and parts of state propaganda, unapologetic joy in committing terrible crimes simultaneously abounds. This gap can be prised open allowing for a counterattack comprising simple public ethical acts.

Recall that more than 1,200 Israeli academics issued an open letter calling on the heads of Israeli academic institutions to 'speak out' and act to stop the war on Gaza. Their letter reads, in part:

> As academics, we recognize our own role in these crimes. It is human societies, not governments alone, that commit crimes against humanity. Some do so by means of direct violence. Others do so by sanctioning the crimes and justifying them, before and after the fact, and by keeping quiet and silencing voices in the halls of learning. It is this bond of silence that allows clearly evident crimes to continue unabated without penetrating the barriers of recognition. . . . We cannot claim that we did not know. We have been silent for too long. For the sake of the lives of innocents and the safety of all the people of this land . . . if we do not call to halt the war immediately, history will not forgive us.[9]

How could this strategy be effective if (most, not all of) the content is already publicly known and proudly assumed by those in power? The difference is the subjective position of enunciation. On 7 November 2024, clashes between football fans at a match between Ajax and Maccabi hit the headlines. Confrontations between Maccabi fans from Israel and pro-Palestinian protesters erupted into violence in the centre of Amsterdam. Even before the match, hundreds of Maccabi Tel Aviv fans patrolled Amsterdam, tearing down Palestinian flags from apartment windows, reportedly shouting obscene slogans like 'There are no schools open in Gaza because we killed all the children!' My response to these appalling rallying cries is just a shift in tone: all we need to do is to repeat exactly the same words but *with shame*. We redeem our human desire by displaying our shame at such acts. What we re-stage is the obscene underside of the Event.

Part 2. Local Turbulences

Dark Humour in the Reign of Daddy Cool

In *I'll Burn That Bridge*, Norman Finkelstein shows his willingness to burn bridges not only with the establishment but also with the mainstream of today's Left: he considers its main tendency

> to have degenerated from soaring moral and intellectual heights with Rosa Luxemburg, W. E. B. DuBois, and Paul Robeson into a censorious, narcissistic, morbidly navel-gazing culture preoccupied with subjectivist trivialities like personal pronouns at the expense of solidaristic struggle for a better world. 'Whenever I see he/him or she/her, I think *fuck/you*,' Finkelstein declares: 'If I can't laugh, I don't want your Revolution.'[1]

This is how I would answer my critics who point out that my bad-taste jokes often imply a racist/sexist position of enunciation that runs against my professed 'progressive' goals. However, what kind of humour are we talking about here? In a recent interview, Peter Sloterdijk kindly praised me for introducing dark humour into philosophy.[2] I think he was right, with the caveat that I don't consider this my personal idiosyncrasy: we live in an age when only dark humour enables us to adequately grasp the madness of our social reality.

Let's take the latest example. On 5 May 2025 the well-known war criminal Benjamin Netanyahu said the population of Gaza would be displaced to a small area in the south of Gaza – in short, to a de facto concentration camp – 'to protect them', Netanyahu said of the 'intensified operation'.[3]

This report cannot but evoke black humour. Israel wants to protect Palestinian lives ... from whom? From Israel itself. First you totally destroy a territory, and then you attack it: the stronger side engages in ethnic cleansing or even in full genocide of its opponent. In such a situation, do we – external observers – have any right to condemn Palestinians for fighting back in the same way as Israel is attacking them, with arms, with terror? But are we – western Europe, in this case – really just external observers? I think the predominant stance of our governments is even worse than that of Israel. The main European countries again and again declare the seriousness of their anxiety about the suffering in Gaza and on the West Bank, but this doesn't prevent them from continuing to supply Israel with arms and working to head off any serious diplomatic actions against it – why? I recently spoke with a couple of high functionaries from different states and parties, and (in deep privacy, of course) I got the same message: of course it is horrible what Israel is doing, it can even be called genocide, but we should realistically accept the sad fact that *ethnic cleansing works* – with clearly delimited borders and ethnic homogeneity, a 'great Israel' may bring peace to the area, so let's let it happen and then accept it as a fact.

So what are we to do in such a situation? The predominant mood among intellectuals is that of resigned pessimism: with the new populism, ideological manipulation has reached such a level that what was once called 'critique of ideology' is today largely inefficient. Cynicism pervades our public spaces to such an extent that the hegemonic ideology is easily able to integrate every criticism into its system as a subordinate moment of its own functioning. Trump is a postmodern obscene clown who doesn't take his own Christian fundamentalist message remotely seriously, he is already a caricature of himself. In the same way, today's Zionists are a perversion, a caricature, of Jewish identity – in what precise way?

Let's make a brief detour and begin with G. K. Chesterton's classic Father Brown story 'The Sign of the Broken Sword', which takes place during a fictional nineteenth-century military conflict between Britain and Brazil. The backstory: General St Clare commanded 800 British infantry in a campaign against the Brazilian general Olivier, a charismatic and generous enemy. St Clare led two or three British regiments in a reckless assault on Brazilian positions, in the course of which his troops suffered heavy casualties and had to surrender. Olivier paroled his prisoners, but soon after, St Clare was found hanging from a tree, his broken sword around his neck. Years later, Father Brown reveals that St Clare, in the course of his military career in India and Africa, engaged in torture, fornication and corruption and ultimately sold British military secrets to the Brazilians. Major Murray, one of St Clare's officers, uncovered the treason and demanded St Clare resign. St Clare murdered him, the point of the general's sword breaking off in the major's body. Coldly calculating, St Clare ordered a doomed assault, making 'a hill of corpses to cover this one'. The surviving British troops are led by Captain Keith who deduced the truth and lynched St Clare as soon as the Brazilians departed.[4]

Is it not the case that Israel is doing the exact opposite of St Clare: focusing on one (or some, i.e., Hamas) to cover the hill of corpses (Palestinians)? No, the Israeli government is doing what St Clare was doing, although with an important shift. It is making a hill of corpses among the Palestinians to cover one corpse – which one? Here comes the surprise: the corpse of Jewish identity. With the majority of Jews in Israel caught in the grip of genocidal logic, they are in some basic sense committing a collective suicide, abandoning the spiritual greatness that characterized their identity. And is Trump not doing the same? His corpse is the corpse of America and democracy ... As I write this, I can already hear 'Leftist' voices shouting back at me that Western 'freedom and democracy' were a hypocritical fake from the beginning, and what is happening now is just the emergence of that core truth. I think this is a simplification which, if we act upon it, can cost us dearly.

So what should the Israeli Jews do if we accept that the two-state solution is a mirage, something that was never taken seriously by any of the people involved? Some of my Palestinian colleagues (like Zahi Zalloua) think that, since the Jews are the colonizers there, the only solution is that they should commit a symbolic suicide: they should radically transform their symbolic identity, abandon their traditional link to the promised land and fully assume their lack of roots. The problem I see with this idea is that caught as they are in a genocidal mania, they (the Zionist Jews) *are already doing this*, committing a symbolic suicide, i.e., abandoning the most precious part of their symbolic legacy. Or, as Yuval Noah Harari (with whom I am definitely not always in agreement) put it:

> Judaism has survived, it has become the world champion in surviving catastrophes. But it has never faced a catastrophe like we are dealing with right now, which is a spiritual catastrophe for Judaism itself. The worst-case scenario that we are facing right now – we can still prevent it – is the potential of an ethnic cleansing campaign in Gaza and the West Bank resulting in the expulsion of two million, maybe more, Palestinians. From there, the establishment of Greater Israel, the disintegration of Israeli democracy and the creation of a new Israel based on an ideology of Jewish supremacy. The worship of what were completely anti-Jewish values for the last two millennia.[5]

One should only supplement these lines with the sad conclusion: the spiritual catastrophe of which Harari speaks is not a sudden event which disturbed authentic Jewishness, its potential was there from the very beginning. Does this mean that there is something especially destructive in Jewish identity itself? No, because we are all part of this story: racism was potentially inscribed into the Enlightenment project; for millennia Jews were the victims of anti-Semitism; the Arab cultures that surround Israel focus on it in order to avoid openly confronting their own antagonisms. In all just criticism of what Israel is doing now, it is absolutely essential to include ourselves into the story. Racism begins the moment we pretend to adopt the role of an innocent observer.

Our basic moral edifice is not just hypocritical (as it always-already was), with the Gaza war it lost even the hypocritical force of appearance – in it and with it, appearance effectively becomes *just an appearance*, no longer an appearance which contains its own truth. Along these lines, Arundhati Roy remarked more than a year ago that, if the bombing of Gaza were to continue, then 'the moral architecture of western liberalism will cease to exist. It was always hypocritical, we know. But even that provided some sort of shelter. That shelter is disappearing before our eyes.'[6] Crucial here is the idea that, in spite of its hypocrisy (or, why not, *because of it* and through it), the liberal moral edifice nonetheless 'provided some sort of shelter'.

DARK HUMOUR IN THE REIGN OF DADDY COOL

So what is replacing the 'moral architecture of western liberalism'? As grudgingly as we want, we have to concede to the devil what appertains to the devil: Donald Trump recently accomplished a series of triumphs. The Supreme Court curtailed the power of federal judges, giving him free hand to rule by decree; his Big Beautiful Bill will make the MAGA vision a legal reality; anti-immigrant measures are being implemented that will target even those who regulated their status in the US and have a legal job there; he has embarked upon a humiliation of Europe, which decided to obey the US suggestion to raise its defence spending, to abandon all dreams of unilaterally recognizing Palestine and to follow the USA's lead in the Middle East conflict; and, finally, Trump succeeded in imposing a ceasefire between Israel and Iran. How did he act in order to achieve this? He abandoned the MAGA dream of focusing on the US and not meddling in conflicts around the world, and assumed the new role of global peacemaker, a peacemaker who doesn't hesitate to impose peace by brutal bombing. He doesn't even pretend to act as equal among equals or as an impartial judge – so what is he?

> NATO made history this week, agreeing to a massive hike in defense spending at its annual summit on Wednesday — but it was the 'bromance' between President Donald Trump and NATO Secretary General Mark Rutte that stole the spotlight. As Trump compared the Middle Eastern adversaries to 'two kids in a school yard' who 'fight like hell,' Rutte interjected, laughing: 'And then daddy has to sometimes use strong language to get them to stop.'[7]

Rutte just forgot to include himself – or, rather, some prominent EU figures – in this list of naughty children who needed to be spanked by a stern but benevolent father: the European states agreed to raise their military spending five per cent only after daddy's severe reprimand. Sadly, this raise did not serve European autonomy but put Europe more than ever under the domination of the US ... Trump thus discovered a new role for himself on a world stage: a global daddy safeguarding peace with a mixture of awards and brutal pressure, including terrorist bombing. He effectively acts as a daddy prone to capricious eccentricities, not constrained by any universally recognized diplomatic rules or even simple rules of common decency, mixing common wisdoms with occasional vulgarities, all of it under the sign of pragmatic realism. And the truly shameful person in this affair is not Trump but all those of us like Rutte who gladly accept this role of unruly adolescents waiting for a severe daddy to control them, and abandon the position they should adopt, that of leaders advocating a principled policy as equal partners in a dialogue. Recall how Trump and Vance humiliated Zelensky in the notorious White House confrontation: while Trump was a daddy cool in his angry mode, rebuking Zelensky for not wanting peace, immediately after the show Zelensky desperately submitted himself to daddy's authority and declared his love for Trump and the US ...

I recall with disgust a hit from my youth, 'Daddy Cool' from 1976 (performed by Boney M),[8] an exemplary case of a musical piece which continues to haunt you with its repetitive stupid enactment of *jouissance*, and the more you try to get rid of it the more it re-emerges – for me, at least, the best musical portrait of Trump. As a daddy, Trump openly prefers one child to another (threatening to turn Tehran to ashes) and his economic policies can be based on this subjective favour (he lowered tariffs for the UK because he likes the country), although one has to admit that in enforcing the ceasefire between Israel and Iran he displayed a certain versatility in allowing the opponent to save face. Recall how Trump thanked Iran for informing the US in advance that they would bomb their military base in Qatar, allowing them to evacuate soldiers and thus prevent any deaths – in spite of all his talk about Iran's unconditional surrender, he understood that, to save its face, Iran must be allowed to make one last attack for which it would not be punished ...

So it is true that Trump, as he says, doesn't want to start conflicts but to end them. However, even if he will succeed in adding other 'triumphs' to his list, there are clear limitations he will encounter in playing a capricious global peacemaking daddy when his opponents simply reject his role of daddy cool. He now promises to bring peace to Gaza – but what can he offer to Palestinians there that would satisfy Israel? As for Ukraine, with an opponent like Putin, the only way open to Trump is to exert even more pressure on Ukraine or to withdraw from his active role – which he is doing now. On the night of 3 July 2025, just hours after the latest Trump–Putin phone call, Russia launched a record number of drones at Ukraine, masses of which were aimed at civilian targets in Kiev. A couple of days earlier, Russia officially admitted that it would deploy 30,000 more soldiers from North Korea to fight against Ukraine. On the same day, Russia moreover became the first nation to recognize the Taliban government of Afghanistan since its 2021 takeover. And Trump? He just made a dry comment on the phone call: 'I didn't make any progress with him [Putin] at all.'[9] However, a day earlier, the Trump administration announced that it would hold back on delivering to Ukraine some air defence missiles, precision-guided artillery and other weapons as part of its pre-stated pause to some arms shipments; this was attributed to American concerns that its own stockpiles had declined too much.[10] A weird welcome for the new wave of Russian attacks, and no role for daddy cool to play here – not to mention China, with which Trump is engaged in true economic warfare.

The problem is that Trump's position of a pragmatic peacemaker, his efforts to deal with problems as if they could be resolved through 'realistic' business negotiations, is a fake: its co-ordinates are predetermined by a whole set of eminently *political* decisions and exclusions. As was the case with Iran, Trump's pragmatic negotiations are just the flip side of a demand for unconditional surrender. Trump as a global daddy cool thus announces a world with no clear rules and no basic ethical principles, a world where the very agent who pretends to control his children caught in violent exchanges acts as a capricious and unpredictable authority. In short, our world is getting closer to a madhouse in which the strongest patient took the reins of power and acts as a doctor.

However, such pessimism, while true up to a point, plays into the hands of those in power. Do we not see on a daily basis how censorship, direct and indirect, is getting stronger than ever? Suffice it to recall how the pro-Zionist network tightly controls what is allowed to appear in our media, relativizing reports on the IDF brutalities into 'alleged' news. More generally, a new type of reporter is appearing, ready to pursue a single issue without constraints, from Julian Assange to Owen Jones – we in the West also have our own Navalnys. The panic they cause in the circles of power is proof that, in spite of all cynical manipulations, telling the factual truth still works. Such figures are our true heroes today, and their sarcastic dark humour is profoundly liberating. However, this sarcastic dark humour is strictly opposed to a very disturbing global pattern which is gradually emerging: the basic social pact binding society together is bursting at its seams. Crazy rumours abound and, even if they're utterly groundless, give voice to our deepest fears and prejudices.

For example, Sergei Markov, a former adviser to Vladimir Putin, expressed his concern that Ukraine was creating 'gay super soldiers' to wage war against Russia:

> Military theorists and historians know which army in Greece was the strongest, remember? The Spartans. They were united by a homosexual brotherhood. They were all homos. These where the politics of their leadership. I think they are planning the same for Ukraine's Armed Forces.[11]

This mixture of homophobia, fake history and the Marvel blockbuster idea of super soldiers is outrageous and unfounded in the extreme and only confirms that Markov doesn't know what thinking is. But things get more dangerous when such deranged ruminations and conspiracy theories involve our biggest historical traumas and crimes. In late August 2023, in a ceremony in the Russian city of Velikiye Lukim, a priest called 'Father Anthony' sprinkled holy water on a twenty-six-foot-high statue of Stalin. He claimed that during Stalin's time in power, 'if we are being honest, the Church suffered', but added that 'thanks to this we have lots of new Russian martyrs and confessors to whom we now pray and are helping us in our Motherland's resurgence'.[12] This line of argument is one step from claiming that Hitler deserves a blessing from Jews because his crimes played a key role in opening up the way to the rise of the State of Israel. Is this a bad joke? Unfortunately not: some Zionist extremists close to the Israeli government openly advocate this stance: 'For years, God has been screaming that the Diaspora is over but Jews aren't obeying. That is their disease that the Holocaust must cure.'[13]

How can we explain the appeal of such perverted arguments? We have to proceed in three steps. First, we should note the counterintuitive fact that, in the developed countries, unrests and revolts have exploded, as a rule, when the rate of poverty is very low – the protests of the 1960s (May '68 in France, anti-Vietnam protests and student riots in the US, etc.) occurred in the golden age of the welfare state. The sad lesson is thus that, if protest is to be avoided, people should not be allowed to live too well: when they live well, they desire even more. Second, we have to take into account the surplus-enjoyment that such perversion gives birth to.[14] Recall the ISIS attack on Crocus City Hall in Moscow on 22 March 2024 where over 130 people were killed – was this also, as some commentators claim, not a terrorist attack but an act of armed resistance, revenge for the massive destruction in Syria caused by the Russian army? (Incidentally, the number of those killed in Crocus City Hall is roughly the same as the number of those killed daily in Gaza.) But something new happened after this attack: while we can safely surmise that all states torture alleged terrorists when captured, Russian security forces not only admitted to this torture but made it public: 'In a graphic video posted on Telegram, one of the detained had his ear cut off and was then forced to eat it by one of his interrogators.'[15] No wonder some Israeli hardliners claim that Russia has shown them how to deal with arrested Hamas members.

Why were they doing it? Not just to scare off potential future attackers but also to give pleasure to the viewers: Margarita Simonyan, a Russian propagandist and head of the state-owned media outlet RT, who shared these pictures, wrote: 'I never expected this from myself, but when I see how they are brought into the court crooked, and even this ear, I feel extremely satisfied.'[16] Why not go even further? Are we gradually returning to the pre-modern practices of publicly torturing alleged criminals to death?

The third step is perhaps the most difficult one; analysing the nature of such surplus-enjoyment. How can people considered 'normal' enjoy such a spectacle, not just as its observers but as its active participants? We are talking here about something that has been practised throughout the entirety of human history, and the answer is: they must be incentivized by some mythic discourse, religion or poetry. Recall how the role of poetry was described by Ernst Jünger, a reluctant Nazi fellow-traveller who, like the Proud

Boys in the US today, celebrated the purifying effect of military struggle: 'Any power struggle is preceded by a verification of images and iconoclasm. This is why we need poets – they initiate the overthrow, even that of titans.'[17]

And the same goes for Israel: on 26 March 2024 *Haaretz* published '"Fire on Your Walls of Gaza": How Israel's Army Uses Revenge Poetry to Boost Morale', a critical report on an anthology published by the IDF including poems which expressed a desire for vengeance and painted the combat in Gaza as a religious war.[18] The call for submissions for the anthology went out on 13 October, and the first volume was published ten days later. The editors invited contributors 'to embark on a poetic journey and reignite the great Israeli spirit', and the collection was intended to 'raise the spirit in wartime', as the IDF defines it.

This is where we find ourselves today. Germany was often called the land of '*Dichter und Denker*' (poets and thinkers), with a turn towards '*Richter und Henker*' (judges and executioners) in authoritarian times. But what if the two versions are more similar than it may initially appear? What if our world is gradually becoming a world of *Dichter und Henker*, of poets and executioners? Brutal violence is increasing all around the world, from Gaza to Sudan, from Ukraine to Colombia, a violence which cannot be justified by any existing legal systems, so that a form of poetry (a mythic narrative not grounded in facts) is needed. To counter this tendency, we need more *Richter und Denker*, more thinkers able to reflect upon our predicament, thereby enabling us to judge properly where we stand and what we can(not) do.

Next Year in Gaza!

My favourite detective novels are those which end with multiple denouements: first the murderer is publicly denounced; then we learn that the true murderer is another person who had framed another suspect; then we learn that both suspects acted together and that there was no murder at all ... The extreme example is not a novel but a film: *Wild Things* (John McNaughton, 1998) which features six successive denouements. The movie follows Sam, a high-school counsellor in South Florida who is accused of rape by two female students, the 'high-class' Suzie and the 'low-class' Kelly. First, we learn that Suzie, Kelly and the counsellor were actually acting together to extort money from Kelly's rich mother, and the twists continue to be unveiled ... And then, at the very end, we learn that Suzie was the ultimate mastermind of the plot – upon finding out that Sam and Kelly were in a sexual relationship. Suzie blackmailed Sam with photographs of the two using drugs during sex, convincing him to help with her scheme. Suzie subsequently orchestrated the meeting between Sam and Ray (the police detective investigating all of this) at a local bar. During her own staged murder on the beach, Suzie pulled out her own teeth with pliers to make her death appear legitimate. Ray shot Kelly first before shooting himself in the shoulder to pretend he killed her in self-defence. Finally, with Kelly, Ray and Sam all dead, Suzie is met by Kenneth, her sleazy defence lawyer, who gives her a briefcase full of cash that he describes as 'just walking around money' and a cheque for millions of dollars. As she leaves, he tells her to 'be good' before taking her drink full of poison, so that Suzie is literally the only survivor.[1]

Apart from its multiple endings, there are two other notable features of *Wild Things*. First, McNaughton commented in 2018 that *Wild Things* was his 'most political film' due to its focus on social class:

> Who wins? The girl from the trailer park! She's all alone on the ninety foot sail boat, out on the Caribbean. Pretty much everyone else is dead. That was the nineties, with the concentration of wealth. But the girl from the trailer park takes 'em all down.[2]

Second, a literary critic, John Thorburn, suggested that the film's 'most under-appreciated element is screenwriter Stephen Peters' obvious debt to classical mythology, tragedy and, especially, two plays by Euripides, *Medea* and *Hippolytus*'.[3] He claims that the character of Suzie is a modern-day version of Medea, while Kelly functions as a Phaedra-like figure, and Sam exemplifies both Jason and Hippolytus. The ancient myth does not provide a key to the deeper meaning of the story. On the contrary, the modern version brings out the repressed truth of the ancient narrative – class struggle.

Of course, one should note at this point that Greek mythologies can be read in endlessly different ways. The tale of Orpheus and Eurydice is a good example – why, on the way back from the underworld, did Orpheus violate the divine prohibition and turn his head back to look at Eurydice, thus losing her forever? What we encounter here is simply the link between the death-drive and creative sublimation: the backward gaze of Orpheus is a perverse act *stricto sensu*, and he loses Eurydice intentionally in order to regain her as the object of sublime poetic inspiration (this idea was developed by Klaus Theweleit).[4] Let's go one step further. What if Eurydice herself, aware of the impasse of her beloved Orpheus, intentionally provoked his turning around? What if her reasoning was something like: 'I know he loves me; but he is potentially a great poet. He cannot fulfill his fate by being happily married to me. The only ethical thing for me to do is to sacrifice myself, to provoke him into turning around and losing me, so that he will be able to become the great poet he deserves to be' – and then she starts gently coughing or something similar to attract his attention ...

Does a similar logic of deferred ending not hold true for Christianity, the only religion which can only be properly understood through a double reversal of the meaning of its key event (the death of Christ on the cross)? To his followers, this death appears as the ultimate catastrophe, the death of God himself, throwing them into utter despair. Then comes the first reversal enacted by Paul: Christ's death is effectively the death *of* death, 'good news', the self-sacrifice of the innocent divinity to emancipate us all, promising a chance of redemption. Interestingly, as regards Christ's ultimate mission/destiny, the character of the wife of Pontius Pilate is interpreted very differently in the Catholic and Protestant traditions. Catholics celebrate her for suspecting that Christ was a holy figure and attempting to convince Pilate not to execute him. I, of course, much prefer the Protestant position: she was an instrument of the Devil. If her husband had capitulated and Christ hadn't died on the cross, his mission would be unfulfilled and there would be no Christianity. In short, the death of Christ was not a tragedy in the standard sense of the word. Christ not only knew he would die but even planned it, effectively ordering Judas (in some tellings, his most trusted follower) to betray him. Judas is the only absolute hero of the Gospels: he forfeited his soul and accepted his legacy as the ultimate figure of treason in order to enable Christ to fulfil his mission.

There is another reversal which follows, although it is ignored even by many Christians. It concerns the topic of the Second Coming. Many Christians understand the return of Christ as a real historical event, believing that at some point in the future, Christ will return to Earth and dwell among us. However, unbeknownst to many believers, this reduces Christ to a pagan messiah. The deepest – and most radical – truth is that the Holy Spirit is *already the second coming*. The community should realize they already have what they are expecting because the love that binds them *is* the Holy Spirit. Therein resides the properly Hegelian core of Christianity: the problem is already its own solution, what we are waiting for already *is*.

So, we have identified similar motifs of reversal in totally different places, in crime cinema, ancient mythology and Christianity. And why, I hear you ask, is this interesting? Because in today's politics we find numerous cases of similar multiple reversals, versions of a detective novel's drawing room – let's just take the case of Israel in the ongoing war in the Middle East (which is far from being the only example). The first story was that, 'out of nowhere', Hamas attacked an

Israeli kibbutz near the Israeli border and a music festival nearby, killing hundreds and taking hostages, etc. Now we know that, although the Hamas incursion is responsible for serious crimes, the story is much more complex. There are multiple indications that Israel not only knew about the attack in advance but was informed by the Egyptian and American secret services, as well as by its own immense spying apparatus (what went on in Gaza was covered by all possible satellite and digital surveillance plus thousands of spies among the Palestinians). In addition, the IDF moved a division protecting the area to the West Bank just two weeks before 7 October. Does this not suggest the possibility that Israel wanted to use the attack as an excuse for waging a war on the people of Palestine?

Plus, it has been reliably reported that in the years before 2023 Israel was amply financing Hamas (through Qatar), although it was aware of Hamas's military activity – the idea was to keep the Palestinians in Gaza politically separated from the Palestinians on the West Bank and thus lessen the pressure on Israel to allow a two-state solution.[5] After the brutal bombardment of Gaza began, many critics of Israel missed the point when they claimed that Israel was failing to achieve its goal of destroying Hamas, instead merely killing thousands of Palestinians and ruining Gaza ... But what if this was their true goal? Not the destruction of Hamas but the ethnic cleansing of Gaza and the West Bank to create a 'Great Israel', from the river to the sea.

The wave of recognitions of the Palestinian state by some big western European countries in 2025, including France and the UK, is marked by a similar ambivalence. Apparently a step in the right direction, clearly limiting Israel's ambitions, at the same time there is a negation included in it – it does what it does in order to avoid doing what really needs to be done to stop the genocidal activity of Israel. To put it another way, as Gideon Levy succinctly does, it is a gift to Israel: 'International recognition of a Palestinian state rewards Israel, which should be thanking each and every country doing so, since such recognition serves as a misleading alternative to what must actually be done – imposing sanctions.'[6] To put it brutally, if we limit ourselves just to recognizing Palestine, there will soon be no Palestinian territory to be recognized as a state. If there will be peace, it will be the kind of peace Trump and

Netanyahu want to impose on Gaza by way of totally destroying it – or, as Tacitus put it two thousand years ago: *ubi solitudinem faciunt, pacem appellant*. ('They make a desolation and they call it peace.')[7]

What is happening in Russia now provides yet another version of the dialectical coincidence of the opposites. Russia has justified its attack on Ukraine by claiming that the Maidan popular uprising was a neo-Nazi *coup d'état*, so that by attacking, Russia is just continuing its long struggle against fascism. Unfortunately, there are details which disturb this clear and simple image. The Wagner Group was controlled by Yevgeny Prigozhin until 2023 and has been used as a proxy by the Russian government, allowing it to have plausible deniability for military operations abroad, especially in Ukraine and in central Africa. Why was it called *Wagner* Group? Because Prigozhin admired Hitler and he chose this name after he discovered that Richard Wagner was Hitler's favourite composer. This group was lately reorganized under the name 'Africa Corps' – here is how Wikipedia describes it:

> The Africa Corps (Russian: *Afrikanskiy korpus*) is a Russian paramilitary group controlled and managed by the Russian government, to support Russian political influence and Russia-aligned governments in Africa. The Corps largely took over the operations of the Wagner Group in Africa, by subsuming and rebranding its structures.[8]

Wikipedia's entry on Africa Corps begins with a disambiguation: *Not to be confused with Afrika Korps*. So what was Afrika Korps? Again, here is the Wikipedia description:

> The German expeditionary force in Africa during the North African campaign of World War II. First sent as a holding force to shore up the Italian defence of its African colonies, the formation fought on in Africa, under various appellations, from March 1941 until its surrender in May 1943. The unit's best known commander was Field Marshal Erwin Rommel, whose reputation as one of the ablest tank commanders of the war earned him the nickname *der Wüstenfuchs*, 'the Desert Fox'.[9]

So although the name was changed, the Nazi connotations remained. The warning '*Not to be confused with Afrika Korps*' is thus simultaneously false and true: true because Africa Corps is not the same as Afrika Korps, false because the whole point of the name 'Africa Corps', just like the name 'Wagner Group', is to evoke the Nazi link. So we cannot say the Nazi connotation was just Prigozhin's private pathology: it is consciously inscribed into the very Russian project of pseudo-autonomous state-financed military groups. And exactly the same holds for the full ethnic cleansing of Gaza planned and gradually but persistently accomplished by Israel and the US: the very fact that, as Israel insists again and again, it is not to be confused with the Nazi genocide of the Jews themselves draws attention to the hidden continuity between the two, to the fact that Germany supports Israel not because it feels responsible for the Holocaust but because it realized that today's Israeli Jews are caught in a spiritual catastrophe that has them abandoning their historical legacy and behave towards Palestinians like the Nazi Germany did towards the Jews.

We have to take a further step here: the stain on the Zionist project, the link between anti-Semites and Zionists, was present from the very beginning. Problems with Israel didn't begin after the 1967 war in which Israel occupied the West Bank, nor even in 1948 when the State of Israel was recognized by the UN. The so-called 'Balfour Declaration' was a public statement issued by the British government in 1917 announcing its support for the establishment of a 'national home for the Jewish people' in Palestine, then an Ottoman region with a small minority Jewish population. The declaration was contained in a letter dated 2 November 1917 from Arthur Balfour, the British Foreign Secretary, to Lord Rothschild, a leader of the British Jewish community, for transmission to the Zionist Federation of Great Britain and Ireland.

The same Balfour, the 'protector of the Jews', presided over the passage of the 1905 Aliens Act, the main objective of which was to limit the entry into Britain of Jews from Eastern Europe (especially from Russia after the pogroms around 1900). The Act did not mention Jews explicitly; it dealt with 'aliens' – foreigners – in general, but 'it is clear that the major purpose of the Act was to stop the flow of East European Jews into Britain'.[10] In short, the movement of Western Jews to Palestine was from the very beginning also an anti-Semitic project. So it shouldn't surprise us that Germany, the perpetrator of Shoah, is the strongest supporter of Israel in Europe – black humour at its absolute darkest.

For almost 2,000 years Jews were spiritually sustained by the famous motto: 'Next year in Jerusalem!' If Palestinians are expelled from Gaza, they will not be able to say 'Next year in Gaza!'. Next year, *there will be no Gaza.*

Sumud: Remember This Word

Public order is disintegrating all over the world, at least according to the media – hardly a day goes by in any country without a dispiriting news story, like the announcement in January 2025 by UK retailers that crime in their stores was 'spiralling out of control' with 55,000 thefts a day and violent and abusive incidents rising by 50 per cent last year.[1] But there is something which should frighten us even more, which is that state authorities participate in rather than preventing this disintegration. Recall the obscenity that exploded in February 2025 when Trump said he would continue funding Ukraine's war effort, but demanded something in return: special access to Ukraine's glut of natural resources, worth around $500bn.[2] Freedom has a price ... in rare minerals.

Such obscenity has reached its peak in the unimaginable horror taking place in Gaza and on the West Bank. True, we should not be in awe of the increasingly wanton violence with which Trump treats Palestinians in Gaza, caught in an immobilizing fascination; but nor should we treat it as an objective fact observed from a safe distance – we should somehow hold on to the shock engendered by its direct shamefulness. If we relinquish this shock, there is nothing to prevent us from shrugging at ethnic cleansing, or even supporting it in a spirit of cynical realism: hey, it works and it's the only way to achieve peace since the past decades clearly show that Palestinians and Jews cannot live together ... If one is thinking in this way, one should go on to ask: why should Palestinians not pursue their dream (or, rather, the dream of some of them) of throwing out the Jews – wouldn't this also bring peace? In other words, if Palestinians are treated like this, do they also not have the right to strike back in any form, including terror?

Trump has said he would like Jordan and Egypt to take in Gazans internally displaced by Israel's devastating war in the enclave: 'You're talking about a million and a half people, and we just clean out that whole thing.'[3] (Note the implication that Palestinians in Gaza are like filth to be wiped out!) The proposal marked a sharp break with the Biden administration's stance on Gaza: it aligns the Trump administration with Israel's most radical far-right politicians who advocate transferring Palestinians out of the territory to make way for Jewish settlements. Trump's proposal was predictably embraced by extremist Israeli politicians, including Finance Minister Bezalel Smotrich – who sparked controversy by claiming there was 'no such thing as a Palestinian people'[4] – and former Minister of National Security Itamar Ben Gvir, who was once convicted (by an Israeli court, no less) for supporting terrorism and inciting anti-Arab racism.

Perspicacious observers quickly noted that Trump's proposal, if it were to materialize, would be self-defeating: destabilizing Egypt and Jordan would strengthen Islamist political forces like the Muslim Brotherhood, which are far less friendly to the US and more sympathetic to Hamas. One cannot but suspect that the pressure on Palestinians in Gaza was part of a secret deal with Israel to accept a ceasefire: the promise of the US was that Israel could achieve what it wanted (a 'clean', empty Gaza) by peaceful means instead of through brutal war.

As usual, the reasoning behind this brutal proposal purports to be humanitarian – Trump said: 'Almost everything is demolished and people are dying there. So I'd rather get involved with some of the Arab nations and build housing at a different location where maybe they can live in peace for a change.'[5] With the use of passive voice so familiar from the media coverage of Gaza, Trump refuses to acknowledge the obvious question: *who* demolished 'almost everything'? None other than those who now enthusiastically support a 'humanitarian' ethnic cleansing. (Needless to add, he also ignores the question of who it was that enabled Hamas to maintain its dominance in Gaza – even though Israel's financial support for Hamas in the late 2010s and early 2020s is now a matter of public record.[6])

The Gaza Palestinians reacted appropriately to this proposal before it was even made, with what they call '*sumud*': a cultural value, ideological theme and political strategy that emerged among the Palestinian people in the wake of the 1967 Six-Day War as a consequence of their oppression and the resistance it inspired. In the late 1970s, *sumud* called for 'a collective third way between submission and exile, between passivity and ... violence to end the occupation'.[7] After the Gaza ceasefire, hundreds of thousands of Palestinians flooded back into northern Gaza after Israel opened military checkpoints that had divided the strip for more than a year. In the dawn light, crowds that had waited by the road overnight began the long walk back to their homes and businesses – or what remained of them – as soon as the crossing opened.[8]

This is *sumud* in practice: a fidelity to one's land which is non-violent but unconditional. Thousands were returning to the ruins because, even if life there was unlivable, these ruins are their home. The message is clear: better to live in tents on the ruins of your home than to suffer another *nakhba*. This rediscovery of belonging to a territory that is one's home gives the lie to the pseudo-Deleuzian topic of 'deterritorialization' that was fashionable some decades ago when proclaiming your territorial roots was instantly denounced as a version of the fascist 'blood and earth' stance. Even today, the new techno-elites are 'deterritorialized', living in a denatured global space, while having a home in the traditional sense is dismissed as lower-class primitivism (with the notable exception of the Jewish claim to the land of Israel). The supreme irony is that the Palestinians' fidelity to their homeland strangely echoes the fidelity of the Jews to their land. But is there not an obvious contradiction between the global character of our life in global neo-feudal society and the fidelity to our local environment? I think the Jewish case is the best example of the coincidence of opposites: Jews who were, for centuries, the most universal of all ethnic groups and as such the instigators of Enlightenment universalism, are now, in their Zionist iteration, totally focused on their territorial claims. Here we see utopia at work: Trump's proposal is 'realistic', Gaza has been made unlivable, and the return of hundreds of thousands to ruins is utopia at its most noble – doing the impossible because the space of our home is destroyed. The conservative commonplace holds that utopias are dystopias in disguise: the attempt to realize utopia necessarily turns it into a nightmare. Indeed, the lesson of post-apocalyptic stories is that the opposite can also hold: a dystopia can be a utopia in disguise. The conclusion to be drawn from this conundrum is obvious and was formulated days after 11 September 2023 by none other than Efraim Halevy, the ex-chief of Mossad, who said in an interview:

> We don't have the luxury to wait. We have to have a viable policy which would deal with the presence in this area of the Jews and the Palestinians. And we are doomed to live together. I don't want to say we are doomed to die together. And if our approach is that we are doomed to live together, we can't simply live together with one part of the equation having the upper part and ignoring the aspirations of the other side.[9]

Ami Ayalon, a former leader of the Israeli security agency Shin Bet, made the point even more succinctly: 'We Israelis will have security only when they, Palestinians, will have hope. This is the equation.'[10] Words for which you may lose your job ... in the free West, that is. What times do we live in when secret police tell truths the public media don't dare to utter! Israel as a whole is paying a heavy price for ignoring this lesson competing with Trump on who will most brutally display raw and arbitrary power without any ethical concerns – or, as Udi Aloni put it, Israel

> has undergone a radical transformation. It has removed its ideological mask and presents pure power for its own sake. Public figures, soldiers, and political leaders openly take pride in brutality – celebrating the suffering of detainees, justifying the murder of women and children, and normalizing genocidal rhetoric. Israel has killed its superego. This is a reversal in the Israeli self-image that is almost impossible for Israelis to grasp, yet obvious to any outside observer. And that is what makes it so disturbing to a humanist Jew.[11]

More precisely, Israel didn't simply renounce its superego – with some irony, we may say that Israeli politics today (and Trumpian populism in general, although they are not the same in their inner structure) openly reassert the superego as defined by Lacan: the pseudo-ethical agency bombarding individuals with the injunction to enjoy. The most disturbing fact is that Israel and the US don't just ignore humanitarian concerns: they evoke them to justify their ethnic cleansing. As Gilles Deleuze wrote decades ago, '*si vous etez pris dans le reve de l'autre vous setez foutu*' (if you are caught in another's dream, you are fucked). This is the sorry fate of Palestinians, ensnared in Trump's dream of a new, happy and peaceful existence where they will be resettled into 'far safer and more beautiful communities', fitted with 'new and modern homes'. According to Trump, such a forced evacuation would give Palestinians 'a chance to be happy, safe, and free'.[12] We know from Stalinism what enforced happiness means – it is certainly not what Palestinians desire. Their desire is made clear on a daily base with *sumud* – an act of pure desire that goes far beyond satisfying one's needs.

As for the brutality of Hamas: yes, of course they have enacted extreme violence at points but their releasing of hostages with dignity and in a good state contrasts blatantly with the lack of information about the state of prisoners, especially woman and children, released by Israel. It is well known that Palestinian prisoners in Israeli jails are tortured horrifically, a fact publicly recognized by debates in the Knesset (the Israeli parliament). How would our media react if we were to learn Israeli hostages held by Hamas were anally penetrated by big metal sticks full of needles so that many of them ended up bleeding to death? And does the destruction of Gaza, which rendered it utterly unlivable (as Trump himself admitted), not also reveal the extent of IDF brutality?

However, does the brutality of Hamas's acts not render irrelevant their claim to some kind of universal humanist perspective, in the same way that Trump's ostensibly humanitarian rhetoric merely cloaks his shocking demand for the displacement of hundreds of thousands of people? No, because *appearances matter*: the fact that Israel no longer cares about appearances is in itself a message about how everything is permitted now and only 'raw' power really matters. Israel is not alone in this: it is just taking what Putin is doing in Ukraine and what Trump is threatening to do in Greenland and Panama to its logical extreme. Welcome to the new world, where there is no one to even try to enforce some minimal global ethical norms and pragmatic compromises are all we have left.

Peace for Our Time

Comparisons between Trump's peace efforts and Chamberlain's proclamation in 1938 that his Munich agreement with Hitler had achieved 'peace for our time' were repeated again and again after the meeting of Trump and Putin in Alaska, conveying the idea that the peace Trump wanted to impose on Ukraine would effectively amount to Ukraine's capitulation to Russia. In a similar way, Trump's claim that he had already ended eight wars was ridiculed. However, I think that Trump's peace efforts should not be dismissed as a ridiculous fake: his mixture of diplomatic activity and the use of brutal military and economic force to stop a war is effectively a model of 'peace for our time', a model of how (economic and military) wars could be and will be ended in our era. After Taylor Swift's triumphant Eras Tour, we now see a no less triumphant Trump peace tour all around the world.

There were two big pieces of news about Donald Trump in October 2025. The first concerned the trade war between the US and China, the second Trump's success in imposing a ceasefire on the Middle East, an act that will strengthen his image of a global peacemaker. These two acts seem to point in opposite directions: Trump as a global peacemaker versus Trump engaged in brutal economic warfare. My claim is that there is no essential difference between the two: in both cases Trump is acting in exactly the same way.

Let's begin with the first act: Trump announced he would impose an additional 100 per cent tariff on goods from China, on top of the 30 per cent tariffs already in effect, starting 1 November or sooner. CNN called the threat a 'massive escalation' after a month-long trade truce between the two nations.[1] Trump's announcement was tied to Beijing ramping up export controls on its critical rare earths, which are needed to produce many electronics, and CNN detailed the impact of the statement on the stock market: 'Markets closed sharply lower on Friday after Trump's initial comments, with the Dow falling by 878 points, or 1.9%. The S&P 500 was down 2.7%, and the tech-heavy Nasdaq tumbled 3.5%.'[2] Was this just a strategic provocation, an excessive decision that is meant to strengthen the position of the US in future negotiations? I suspect Trump himself isn't sure about it – he simply plans to see how the situation develops ... A sudden and unexpected volte-face is one of Trump's trademarks, not to mention his advocacy of inconsistent political moves: after advising the EU to respond aggressively to incursions by Russian drones, he moves to a renewed friendly dialogue with Putin. If one pursues this logic to its extremes, one can well imagine a local war between the EU and Russia in eastern Europe while the construction of a direct undersea rail link between Russia and the US goes on. Trump now provides more arms to Ukraine, but (as he likes to point out) they are paid for by EU states ...[3] Trump does business like war and war like business.

One detail from the short open conflict between the US and Iran says it all. It was reported by *Truthout* that on 22 June 2025, Iran fired retaliatory strikes against the US, targeting an American military base in Qatar with 'the same number of missiles the US had dropped on Iran during its unprovoked attack a day earlier'. The US reaction? Trump said

> that Iranian officials provided the U.S. with advance notice of the strike. He struck an optimistic tone in a post on Truth Social shortly after.... Trump called the strikes 'very weak' and thanked Iran for giving notice. He appeared to insinuate that the tit-for-tat strikes between the U.S. and Iran were over. 'I am pleased to report that NO Americans were harmed, and hardly any damage was done. Most importantly, they've gotten it all out of their "system", and there will, hopefully, be no further HATE. I want to thank Iran for giving us early notice, which made it possible for no lives to be lost, and nobody to be injured,' said Trump.[4]

This reaction also displays an awareness of how, if one wants peace, one should give the enemy a chance to save face, but there is also a hidden humiliation in it: such an act of thanking, if performed *publicly*, annihilates the dimension of saving the enemy's face.

Until now the supreme act of Trump's peacemaking was the ceasefire in Gaza, and, as numerous commentators were quick to note, what is not mentioned in the peace treaty is almost more important than what is mentioned in it, beginning with the fate of the West Bank. However, I think it is wrong to merely point out these blanks and interpret them as signals that Israel will get everything it wants in a roundabout way. The lacunae in the agreement open up a possible space of struggle. Yes, Trump ignored Palestinians in his 'negotiations' which were sustained by a brutal pragmatic pressure and strategic calculation with no sense of justice. The deal was made between the US and the pro-US Arab countries (Egypt, Saudi Arabia, the United Arab Emirates plus Turkey), and it was only afterwards that Trump put pressure on Israel to accept it, conceding that Gaza would not become part of Israel but – in the long term, at least – would be governed by Palestinians themselves.

Trump was not, of course, a neutral mediator: he put pressure on Israel because he was aware that his project of peace fits in better with the long-term interests of Israel than the 'Great Israel' project pursued by the Israeli extremist government. Trump said that if Hamas didn't uphold the ceasefire deal, Israeli forces could resume fighting in Gaza 'as soon as I say the word',[5] knowing very well that the IDF was already violating the terms of the deal. This radical partiality on Trump's part becomes clearly visible if we take a quick look at the list of the Palestinians set free by Israel and focus on those who were *not* on the list. The absence of two names stands out: Marwan Barghouti, the 'Palestinian Mandela' who is now in prison serving four life sentences. Although his Palestinian credentials are impeccable, he advocates negotiations with Israel and the two-state solution, plus he is the only Palestinian figure who can beat Islamist radicals in elections – that's why he presents a much greater danger to Israeli radical Zionists than Hamas. The second figure is Abu Safiya, director of the Kamal Adwan Hospital in northern Gaza, who has been arrested and imprisoned without charge by Israel since 27 December 2025.[6] Safiya was risking his life on a daily basis to treat patients – figures like him will be desperately needed if Palestinians will ever be allowed to run their own lives in Gaza.

Gaza and the West Bank are now like Croatia at the time of the civil war between Croatia and Serbia in ex-Yugoslavia in the early 1990s, with the Yugoslav army supporting the Serbs. There was a joke circulating among English-speaking Western reporters at that time: 'Tudjman (the president of Croatia) wants peace in Croatia, Milošević (the Serb leader) wants a piece of Croatia, and the Army bombing Croat towns wants to piss on Croatia.' In today's Middle East, Palestinians want peace, the Israeli majority wants a piece of the occupied territories at least, and the murderous neo-fascist Zionists want to piss on Palestinians...

The Trumpian peace means that the genocide in Gaza will be treated as if it didn't happen or, if it is mentioned at all, it will sound in a way that acts as a paraphrase of Brecht's saying from his *Beggar's Opera*: 'What is the robbing of a bank compared to the founding of a new bank!' Now we can say: 'What is the illegal murder of a couple of hundred Jews compared to the legitimate self-defence of Israel (which involves a full genocide)?' This should absolutely not be allowed: what Israel is doing in the occupied territories should be forever inscribed into our historical memory, exactly like the Holocaust. Whatever will happen, not only Netanyahu but also most of the leaders of the 'free West', from Starmer to Merz, including Trump himself, should be stigmatized for what they are: war criminals. Trump's 'peace for our time' is one in which perpetrators of a genocide will continue to be celebrated as peacemakers.

In Israeli political life today, there is a figure similar to Barghouti and Abu Safiya, the Hadash Party head Ayman Odeh who was ousted from the Knesset during Trump's speech on 13 October 2025 because he held up a sign that read 'Recognize Palestine'.[7] Odeh was called an agent provocateur, but Hadash is the only party in Israel which includes Palestinian and Jewish members. It advocates cooperation between Palestinians and Jews, and it is this very moderate stance which has made Odeh the most hated person in Israel, much more hated than the 'terrorists' ... With regard to the ceasefire treaty, Odeh insists that, although this treaty is extremely unjust, it at least opens up a window of hope that the unbearable suffering of the Palestinians in Gaza will be eased. In his interviews, he emphasizes that the first task today is simply to do everything possible to stop the genocidal violence to which Palestinians are submitted.[8] And we should adopt the same position towards Trump's ongoing peacemaking in Ukraine: if it will lead to any result, it will be without doubt an unjust and brutally pragmatic peace, but it will be a peace that will enable Ukrainians to get out of the nightmarish situation in which they are trapped, to take a respite and make a series of difficult decisions.

But am I not talking here like Trump who recently wrote apropos the Ukraine-Russia war: 'It is time to stop the killing, and make a DEAL! Enough blood has been shed'[9]? Putin said the same thing a couple of times, with the addition of blaming Ukraine for the bloodshed. Let's not forget that aggressors are, as a rule, in favour of peace – peace means, for them, the opportunity to enjoy the fruits of their occupation and denounce any resistance to their occupation as 'warmongering'. After Hitler occupied most of Europe in 1940, he definitely wanted peace in the occupied territories, and de Gaulle's message to the French people in 1940 was precisely the insistence that 'No, the war is not over!' Hitler's offer of a peace treaty to Great Britain in 1940 was undoubtedly sincere, and he was deeply disappointed when Churchill rejected it, promising the British people blood, sweat and tears. So there is no principled *a priori* answer to the dilemma of when to accept an enforced, unjust peace: it depends on circumstances. One thing is clear, however: when peace is signed on the gigantic pile of bones of a genocide and confirms the victory of its perpetrators, it is, to turn around von Clausewitz's famous definition of war, just a continuation of war by other means. And the defeated side has not only the right but also the duty to act in the same way: to use peace in order to continue its fight with other (political, cultural, economic) means.

However, Trump did not just redefine peace for our time, he also redefined war: it is as if the war which Trump endeavours to squash in international relations is returning with a vengeance within the US itself. The supreme irony here is that Trump's peacenik image sits at odds with his warlike perception of the situation within the USA itself. Now that the conflict between Trump and Elon Musk, the face of techno-Trumpism, has imploded and Musk has (temporarily, in all probability) withdrawn, it's time to focus on the other pole of Trump's polarized universe, Steve Bannon's 'Left' populism. Apropos of the use of National Guard and US marines in LA against protestors, Bannon proposed a simple and shocking answer to the obvious question: how could Trump's deployment of marines on US soil be justified when the US Constitution holds that armed forces can only be used in conflict against an external enemy? His answer was that the US *is* at war, that World War III had begun in California with the mass pro-immigrant protests:

> The Trump administration will use its legal powers to bust up the monopolistic power of Big Tech. We're going to break up Facebook. We're going to break up Google. We're going to break up Amazon. We're going to break . . . I think hopefully we get to eventually break up Walmart. You've got too much concentration of private power. It's obvious it's anti-populist. It's anti-economic nationalist.[10]

Bannon then takes a step further and – in quite a correct 'Marxist' way – establishes a link between concentrated private power and the state power which serves the first: the protesters

> are calling for unrest nationwide. And it's already expanded to San Francisco. The question here is, who told the police to step down? I think there's only ten arrests. The LAPD allowed that thing to metastasize. Who gave the order? Whoever. Whoever was the government official that gave that order should be arrested this morning. We need to start arresting government officials, including the Mayor of Los Angeles, Karen Bass, who's stirring this pot up. If that means suspending habeas corpus, so be it.[11]

Bannon's proposed list of arrests includes Gavin Newsom, the California governor – Trump himself said he was considering Newsom's arrest.[12] The ongoing protests are certainly not a sign of the president's weakness: he *actively* solicits them so that the US can become a de facto dictatorship. On 30 September 2025, Defense Secretary Pete Hegseth gave a long, weird speech in Quantico to the entire top brass of the US army flown there from all around the world, deploying his vision for how the US military will physically look and act, and offering a stark conclusion: 'If you don't agree, resign.' The right policies, according to Hegseth, centre on his broader campaign against past efforts that he has deemed 'woke', aimed at promoting diversity or accommodating troops – the specifics of which were made official in ten directives sent out to military leadership as he spoke. Hegseth decreed that there would be no 'fat troops' or 'fat generals and admirals in the halls of the Pentagon', that troops would be clean-shaven, that the military would offer few if any exemptions, either for religious or medical needs, and that there would only be male physical standards for combat jobs. If that meant there were no women in those roles, 'it is what it is' . . .[13]

As anonymously noted by many officers who were present, this image of a soldier is much more theatrics than the faithful rendering of the army life 'as it is'. Hegseth's wish to get 'real soldiers' resuscitates an old image of a soldier that has no place in today's wars fought by drones and rockets mostly controlled by geeks behind a screen, and in today's world where we were just informed about the first AI-generated actress, 'Tilly Norwood', who already appeared as the star in the AI-generated comedy sketch 'AI Commissioner' and in various promotional and social media content.[14] Paradoxically, Hegseth's figure of a soldier is a masculine version of Tilly Norwood, an imagined fake we could call 'Till Norwood'. However, more important than this fantasy is Hegseth's description of what these new soldiers should be doing:

> We unleash overwhelming and punishing violence on the enemy. We also don't fight with stupid rules of engagement. We untie the hands of our warfighters to intimidate, demoralize, hunt and kill the enemies of our country. No more politically correct and overbearing rules of engagement. This administration has done a great deal from day one to remove the social justice, politically correct and toxic ideological garbage that had infected our department, to rip out the politics, no more identity months, DEI offices, dudes in dresses. No more climate change worship, no more division, distraction, or gender delusions. No more debris.[15]

It is a coincidence, but an important one, that this event took place days after Vladimir Putin signed the law on Russia's withdrawal from the European Convention for the Prevention of Torture and Inhuman or Degrading Treatment or Punishment. The EU responded:

> The formal decision is one more step in Russia's complete disengagement from its international commitments and clearly demonstrates Russia's disregard for the protection of human rights. It has not allowed any monitoring visits to places of deprivation of liberty. The primary victims of the decision are and will be Russian citizens. According to the UN Special Rapporteur on the situation of human rights in the Russian Federation, 'torture and other cruel, inhuman or degrading treatment or punishment are used as state sanctioned tools for systemic oppression in the Russian Federation'.

And, of course, in Ukraine.[16] Torture legitimized – this is the Russian version of what happens when 'we untie the hands of our warfighters to intimidate, demoralize, hunt and kill the enemies of our country' . . .

And who are these enemies? After Hegseth, Trump himself took the stage and, in an even longer and more rambling speech, proposed using American cities as training grounds for the armed forces. His central claim was that the US needs its military might to combat what he called the 'invasion from within', a phrase used in anticipation by Bannon in his justification of the use of US marines against the protesters in LA:

> We should use some of these dangerous cities as training grounds for our military. We're under invasion from within. No different than a foreign enemy but more difficult in many ways because they don't wear uniforms.[17]

We have known this for months – Trump plans to use the armed forces to 'discipline' big cities which are under the control of the Democratic Party (not just LA but also Chicago, New York, New Orleans . . .). Part of this plan is also to bring to trial and arrest big names from the Democratic Party like Barack Obama and Gavin Newsom – in short, the plan is to criminalize political opponents, to transform political struggle into direct legal and military oppression. In the legal sphere, Trump is making purges that would bring a smile to Stalin's face. Difficulties arise, however, when it comes to the armed forces. While the usual strategy of Rightist populism is to risk an external war to enforce internal patriotic unity, Trump is now doing almost exactly the opposite. In global politics he presents himself as a big peacemaker (boasting that he has stopped seven wars, trying to enforce peace in Ukraine and the Middle East), although his peacemaking is as a rule sustained by brutal local military interventions or at least military threats (such as promising Gaza 'hell' if they don't accept his peace plan).[18] However, within the US he perceives the situation is that of a war to the death, which demands the use of the US army ...

This paradox doesn't necessarily lead to catastrophe: in today's crazy world it may work, for a time at least. The problem resides elsewhere. Until now, it seemed that special units of the National Guard under Trump's direct control would be able to do the job, functioning like the president's private army which he could use wherever he decides, outside any political control. Now Trump has made a crucial step further: the National Guard alone is not enough to deal with the enemy within, so one has to politicize the regular army itself. If one listens to Hegseth's and Trump's speeches, the first thing that strikes the eye (or, rather, the ear) is the *silence* of the gathered generals and admirals: no applause interrupting the speakers, no vivid reaction ... This silence is easy to understand: while clearly an instrument of American global politics, the US army, especially its top generals, passionately wants to protect its image of political neutrality, of avoiding getting caught in political struggles, of respecting the Constitution and obeying only legal orders. This is why, back in 2019 when Trump lost his bid for re-election and repeatedly stated that Biden was not legally president, making (not always) veiled calls to his supporters to openly rebel against the state power, army leaders publicly declared that they were ready to intervene to prevent public disorder, i.e., if there were attempts to bring Trump back to power by unconstitutional means. If we follow this train of thought to its ultimate conclusion, we should consider the possibility that, if Trump were to go all the way in his project of using armed forces to fight the enemy within, the US army might feel compelled to intervene directly and topple Trump. A breathtaking prospect: will a military coup save us from Trump dictatorship?

But there is much more to this question of the army's role in public life. One often hears today that the Left lacks the positive vision of a viable alternative to Trumpian populism – caught in rehashing old models, mainly those of the social democratic welfare state, the Left fails again and again to make a meaningful impact. So what if we take a risky step and abandon the fear of militarization that is a permanent feature of all Leftist utopias? What if we imagine a utopia of the complete militarization of society as the only realistic emancipatory vision? Before dismissing this as a cheap postmodern paradox, remember that Fredric Jameson did exactly this in his *American Utopia*.[19] The idea came to him when, during the 1952 US presidential elections, the Democrat Adlai Stevenson advocated universal free healthcare, and Dwight Eisenhower snapped back: 'If you want free healthcare, join the army!' Jameson's response was to wonder why, then, someone did not propose the army as the universal model for a society.

Jameson dismisses not only the two main forms of twentieth-century state Socialism (the social democratic welfare state and the Stalinist Party dictatorship) but also the very standard by means of which the radical Left usually measures the failure of the first two, the libertarian vision of Communism as a free association of the social multitude organized in councils, i.e., as anti-representational direct democracy based on citizens' permanent engagement. Measured by this standard, global militarization is, of course, unacceptable to our ordinary democratic sensibilities – no wonder that, in a CUNY debate with Jameson, Stanley Aronowitz desperately tried to reduce Jameson's utopian idea of universal conscription back to the model whereby people (soldiers) organize themselves in councils, like the first 'soviets' and other such revolutionary armies. Such direct democracy is the extreme manifestation of the politicization of an entire society, while Jameson repeatedly emphasizes that his idea of universal conscription aims at the disappearance of the political dimension as such: all that remains in Jameson's utopian society is a militarily (i.e., non-politically) organized economy with no need for the permanent engagement of the people, and the immense (and also non-political) domain of cultural pleasures, from sex to art.

As Jameson points out, what makes this model attractive is precisely the impenetrable passive-bureaucratic aspect of the army life: there are no democratic public elections in it – it is never quite clear how one person becomes a top general and not another ... A very stupid counter-argument against Jameson's utopia often raises its head, asking: but doesn't the existence of an army presuppose the threat of war, at least? The answer is clear: our very survival is threatened by the ecological crisis, the exploding domination of AI, not to mention the actual outbreak of a global war. In each of these situations (and especially in their combination), a strong centralized power will be needed, a power ready to act, unencumbered by long and complex democratic procedures. In such a situation, not only an army-like structure but a strong leader at its top will be needed – why?

What characterizes a true leader is, among other things, the ability to make tough decisions where they cannot be avoided: which group of soldiers to sacrifice on a battlefield, which patient to let die when there are not enough resources, etc. – or, as an old doctor in the TV series *New Amsterdam* says: 'Leaders make choices that keep them awake at night. If you sleep well, you are not one of them.' Paradoxically, the excess that cannot be captured by mechanisms of electoral political representations can only find an adequate expression in a leader or a leading body which is able to impose a long-term social and economic project and is not constrained by the narrow period between two elections ... Does this sound like universal militarization? Yes – the forthcoming Communism will be a war Communism or there will be none.[20]

The Story of Three Faces

We are daily bombarded by grisly details of the horrors in Gaza, Ukraine, Sudan ... no wonder we are gradually becoming insensitive to this type of news, their horrors losing the power to shock us. Ten children killed in Gaza – so what? Yesterday it was twenty! Long analyses are also getting repetitive and boring: although new details are appearing all the time, like clear signs that Israel knew about the forthcoming 7 October attack and allowed it to justify the creation of 'Great Israel', analyses basically retell the same story again and again (for the simple reason that the same story *is* happening again and again). So what if we change our approach and focus on an apparently minor detail which, like a Freudian symptom, reveals a lot about our global situation: the expression of the faces accidentally caught on the camera, the faces of those who are part of the ongoing horrors.

Let's begin with the weird, shifting facial expressions of Putin when he appeared with Trump in front of the press at the end of their Alaska meeting, as journalists shouted questions (mainly about the war in Ukraine) and tried to catch their attention of the two war criminals.[1]

The first thing that strikes the eye is the contrast between Putin and Trump who stands at his side – it is as if they exchanged their usual roles. Trump is much more subdued, trying to maintain some kind of dignified appearance as a serious negotiator, while Putin seems relaxed, pulling faces that express anger, then laughter. This is how the clear winner of the summit behaves: slightly annoyed, not really caring about appearances, while Trump desperately acts as if he is a partner in a dialogue of equals – this is, to borrow Trump's own term, how a loser acts. Putin's triumph is clearly signalled by the fact that Trump, the alleged neutral mediator in the

THE STORY OF THREE FACES

conflict, said in one of his later reactions that 'peace now depends on Ukraine'.[2] Another thing to note is that even though no substantial change followed the summit, Putin was not only received as the leader of a superpower but obviously succeeded in re-establishing a camaraderie with Trump that is totally missing when he meets Zelensky or western European leaders. For Putin, Trump was certainly not a 'daddy cool' mediating between the two sides of the conflict. Although Trump pretended to act as an ally of

Ukraine and the EU trying to make a deal with the common enemy, his *actual* behaviour was, as we have already established, that of the gangster patriarch who had made the deal with his ambiguous enemy-partner and was now engaged in making his unruly children recognize this pact.

But we are here at the highest level of world leaders/war criminals, so let us pass to a criminal who acts as an ordinary woman with no political links – Daniella Weiss, the 'godmother' of the West Bank settlers who has, for decades, organized the occupation of Palestinian land. In her interview with Piers Morgan, she refused to express even a minimal compassion for the 20,000 Palestinian children murdered in Gaza[3] – her goal is that the whole of Gaza and the West Bank should be cleansed of all Palestinians on the basis that the land was given by God to the Jews. There is nothing new and original in this message – the true horror comes from how she acts while she is saying this, her face mixing faked naivety with primitive cunning, while accompanying most of her talk with a broad smile, as if she is doing the most ordinary thing imaginable. She is so perfect in this role that sometimes she caricatures herself – one finds it difficult to believe that such a flawless combination of evil and disingenuousness can exist. This is not Hannah Arendt's 'banality of Evil': Daniella is not a cold bureaucrat, she fully enjoys her evil.

When, in an interview with Louis Theroux, she explains the strategy of expanding settlements, her description of how settlers relate to the Israeli state power cannot but strike us as pure and simple truth:

> We do for governments what they cannot do for themselves. Even if you take Netanyahu now, who is very happy about what we do here and also [about] our plans to build a Jewish community in Gaza. He's happy about it but he cannot say it. He says the opposite. It's not realistic. Good! We will make it realistic. It's not forcing the government. It's helping the government. It's step number one in politics. You don't force the government. You [give] the government the ability, the courage, the public support, the political support.[4]

And she sees this strategy as a continuation of the founding of Israel itself: first, they gradually built settlements in Palestine, and when there were enough settlements and the geopolitical situation had changed in the right ways, their formal organizations demanded their territory be recognized as a state ... Crucial here is the duplicity between the civic movement (of settlers) and the official public policy of state organs: the civic movement does what the state officially denies it wants and even condemns, and in this way gradually creates conditions for the state to accept what is already a fact ... Moreover, one cannot but note that the 'democratic' West is now doing exactly the same: officially it is condemning the ethnic cleansing of Gaza and the West Bank, but it is silently tolerating it, i.e., not taking any serious measures against it and even supporting Israel, just waiting for the moment when the mask will fall and it will be able to openly accept the situation on the ground ('Great Israel') ... No wonder a group of Jewish academics officially proposed Daniela Weiss as a candidate for the next year's Nobel Peace Prize.[5]

And what about the faces of her victims, those she refuses to feel any compassion for? Instead of the usual photos of starving children and bodies in ruined buildings, I've chosen the emaciated face of Marwan Barghouti when he was briefly visited in his solitary cell by none other than Itamar Ben-Gvir, the Israeli minister of security who was once condemned for racism by the State of Israel itself. In a brief video clip that Ben-Gvir himself put on the web,[6] we see him threateningly addressing Barghouti, who has spent over twenty years in prison serving four life sentences without losing his popularity among the Palestinians – no wonder he is often referred to as the Palestinian Mandela. If you compare Barghouti's appearance in this clip with photos of him from earlier years, the difference is shocking: once bursting with energy, now he is literally a shadow of himself, an emaciated old man without hair, wobbling helplessly and unable to speak – obviously a victim of systematic starvation and torture.

So why did Ben-Gvir make this humiliating clip public at precisely this moment? The reason is clear: it is a reaction to the fact that many key western European countries have made known

their intention to recognize the state of Palestine, and Barghouti is the key figure in the two-state solution – again, why?[7] One of the few surprising voices of reason in Israel is Ami Ayalon, former leader of Shin Bet, who said back on 14 January 2023: 'We Israelis will have security only when they, Palestinians, will have hope. This is the equation.'[8] Ayalon argued that the Israeli authorities should release Barghouti, jailed leader of the second intifada, to direct negotiations to create a Palestinian state:

> Look into the Palestinian polls. He is the only leader who can lead Palestinians to a state alongside Israel. First of all because he believes in the concept of two states, and secondly because he won his legitimacy by sitting in our jails.[9]

In short, Barghouti is the only person who can beat Hamas in a free election on the West Bank and in Gaza, In contrast to Hamas, he advocates a peaceful two-state solution, while in contrast to the Palestinian Authority on the West Bank which is corrupted and totally under Israeli control, he retains full political independence. That's why he should remain in jail (or maybe even liquidated) if Israel is to realize its goal of radical ethnic cleansing of the Palestinian territories organized by Daniella Weiss.

Part 3. The Black Hole of Our World

Let's Pray Trump Survives

Liberal critics regularly chastise Trump for his dictatorial style full of improvised contingent decisions. He proclaimed a state of emergency which allowed him to rule through executive orders, bypassing Congress and Senate, as well as pointless debates with members of his own party. It is true that he runs the show as a monarch, but I don't think this is a problem – the problem is the nature of the measures he is imposing. In our epoch when the standard multiparty liberal democracy repeatedly displays its inability to cope with the catastrophic prospects we are all confronting, and when more and more people are escaping into apolitical depression, a dictatorial figure, a new master, is needed:

> The master is the one who helps the individual to become subject. That is to say, if one admits that the subject emerges in the tension between the individual and the universality, then it is obvious that the individual needs a mediation, and thereby an authority, in order to progress on this path. The crisis of the master is a logical consequence of the crisis of the subject. One has to renew the position of the master, it is not true that one can do without it, even and especially in the perspective of emancipation. This capital function of leaders is not compatible with the predominant 'democratic' ambience, which is why I am engaged in a bitter struggle against this ambience (after all, one has to begin with ideology).[1]

We have to fully accept this fact: left to ourselves, we are not free but enslaved to our spontaneous prejudices manipulated by the mass media. A master is needed, not so much to tell us what we want, what is *really* good for us, but to deliver a simple message: 'You can!' You can reach beyond yourself and make what appears impossible possible. The majority – me included – *wants* to be passively relying on an efficient state apparatus to guarantee the smooth running of the entire social edifice, so that I can pursue my work in peace. Walter Lippmann wrote in his *Public Opinion* (1922) that the herd of citizens must be governed by 'a specialized class whose interests reach beyond the locality' – this elite class is to act as a machinery of knowledge that circumvents the primary defect of democracy, the impossible ideal of the 'omni-competent citizen'.[2]

This is how our democracies function – with our consent. There is no mystery in what Lippmann was saying, it is an obvious fact; the mystery is that, in full knowledge of what's going on, we play the game anyway. We act *as if* we are free and freely deciding, silently not only accepting but even *demanding* that an invisible injunction (inscribed into the very form of our free speech) tells us what to do and think. Which is why a proper politician does not only advocate people's interests: it is through him that they discover what they 'really want'. In order for the individuals to 'reach beyond themselves', to break out of the passivity of representative politics and engage themselves as direct political agents, the reference to a leader is necessary, a leader who allows them to pull themselves out of the swamp like Baron Munchhausen.

Was Franklin Delano Roosevelt not precisely such a leader? He largely ignored Congress and made decisions relying on a narrow circle of advisers; he tried to directly address and mobilize the people (remember his evening live radio addresses). Although there are obvious differences between Roosevelt and Trump,[3] I think they both acted similarly, each imposing a radical break in the functioning of US society: Roosevelt's New Deal, Trump's MAGA. The two, of course, moved in opposite directions: what Trump is now doing is to a large extent the undoing of the welfare state created by Roosevelt, which resulted in major industrial growth as well as the provision of help to other countries (such as the Marshall Plan after World War II) which made the US even richer. Roosevelt was also a 'militarist' who, against the opinion of the majority who opposed becoming involved in another European war, dragged the US into the war.

While we should remain opposed to Trump more than ever, we should be fully aware of what he is doing. In the four years he was out of power, he learned the Leninist lesson: organize a movement, establish a plan, gradually take over positions, following Stalin's wisdom that 'cadres decide everything'.[4] Let's take the tariffs imposed by Trump: they are not as crazy as they appear. Yanis Varoufakis and others have clearly demonstrated how they are part of a long-term plan to lower the value of the dollar and re-industrialize the country to give a boost to exports, while making sure that the US dollar remains universal currency. Trump is thus announcing the third stage of capitalism after World War II, following Bretton Woods in 1944 and the neoliberal era in 1971 when Nixon relaxed the gold coverage of the US dollar – we should always remember that both these stages were also imposed by the US. In the neoliberal era, US prosperity was based on the negative trade balance of the US: the import from countries with lower wages guaranteed low prices plus enabled the US to profit from dollarization – dollars which other countries got for exporting to the US largely remained there (foreign countries buying properties and investing on Wall Street).

After the 2008 financial crisis, the neoliberal model became untenable; Trump understood this and conceived a way out which will not necessarily fail – only a concentrated effort of other big economies can break the US hegemony, but Trump's 'chaotic' tariffs aim at preventing this by way of negotiating for lower tariffs with each country separately. All one can say is that the non-economic biases of Trump's tariffs are clear: on 2 April 2025 Trump unveiled tariffs of at least 10 per cent on virtually the entire world, even an Arctic island inhabited solely by penguins, with one notable exception: Russia.[5] But it's not just the potential for economic chaos that should perturb us, it is the deliberate dismantling of the global ethico-political order. The US and many other states are serially committing (or participating in) war crimes which they less and less even attempt to justify with fake excuses – you just do it because you can do it, so the whole world is gradually 'Trumpisized', normalizing previously unacceptable brutalities.

Here is a 'minor' example. On 24 March 2024, Israeli settlers brutally beat up Hamdan Ballal, one of the Palestinian co-directors of the Oscar-winning documentary *No Other Land*, in front of his house in the West Bank village of Susiya. The IDF unit which had been present throughout and even helped the settlers terrorize

Ballal then arrested Ballal, not any of the settlers. According to Ballal's attorney, Lea Tsemel, police informed her that he was being held at a military base for medical treatment. However, the next morning she was still unable to reach him and had no further information on his whereabouts. After twenty hours' detention (with no medical treatment), Ballal was released with no explanation . . .[6] The message was clear: this is now a reign of terror with no public authority on which one can rely for protection.

But if Trump refuses to denounce such a state of things, what do I mean by saying that we should pray that Trump lives a long life? It's very simple: if Trump dies soon, J. D. Vance will take over, and I think Vance is a much more dangerous figure than Trump. Let us reach back into history and recall the relationship between the SA and the SS during the rise of Nazism, and the class and ideological tensions between them. The SA, the original street bullies of the Nazis, were thugs, ex-enlisted soldiers who came from the working classes, seen as sleazy, dirty guys who enjoyed torturing their victims. The SS came later, and their members looked down on the SA as common bullies; an SS member was, on the contrary, a cold professional who performed his unspeakable acts in an impersonal way, for the sake of duty:

> Behind the blind bestiality of the SA, there often lay a deep hatred and resentment against all those who were socially, intellectually, or physically better off than themselves, and who now, as if in fulfilment of their wildest dreams, were in their power. This resentment, which never died out entirely in the camps, strikes us as *a last remnant of humanly understandable feeling*. The real horror began, however, when the SS took over the administration of the camps. The old spontaneous bestiality gave way to an absolutely cold and systematic destruction of human bodies, calculated to destroy human dignity; death was avoided or postponed indefinitely. The camps were no longer amusement parks for beasts in human form, that is, for men who really belonged in mental institutions and prisons; the reverse became true: they were turned into 'drill grounds', on which perfectly normal men were trained to be full-fledged members of the SS.[7]

Hyperbolic though it might sound, the same holds for Trump and Vance. Trump remains somewhat human in his vulgar-obscene brutality, while Vance is a robotic manipulator created and dominated by Peter Thiel. The reign of Trumpian obscenity will not exist forever: a clown (Trump, Musk) is needed to establish a new feudal regime, and once this regime begins to function on its own, the cold, hard robots (Vance, Thiel) can openly take over. We will no longer have oppression as a clownish joke but oppression unfiltered and unfettered. No wonder that, in an executive order signed on 27 March 2025, Trump put Vance in charge of stopping government spending on 'exhibits or programs that degrade shared American values, divide Americans based on race, or promote programs or ideologies inconsistent with Federal law and policy'. This order targets the Smithsonian Institution, the world's largest museum complex:

> Once widely respected as a symbol of American excellence and a global icon of cultural achievement, the Smithsonian Institution has, in recent years, come under the influence of a divisive, race-centered ideology. This shift has promoted narratives that portray American and Western values as inherently harmful and oppressive.[8]

It is crucial that we properly locate this direct act of censorship, worthy of the darkest Stalinist purges which were directed at 'bourgeois cosmopolitanism': it is definitely not just a simple regression from the anti-racist and feminist achievements of political correctness. It is rather their *symptom*, the brutal emergence of what was effectively wrong in what Trumpians designate as the insanity of PC. The constellation which predominated until the rise of the new Rightist populism was best described by Jean-Claude Milner,[9] who posited that what we call 'the West' is today a confederation under US hegemony; the US reigns over us intellectually as well, but here 'one has to accept a paradox: the US-American domination in the intellectual domain expresses itself in the discourses of dissent and protest and not in the discourses of order'. The global university teaches us

> to refuse the economic, political, and ideological functioning of the western order in part or entirely. Inequality plays the role of

an axiom, from which all ultimate criticism derives. Depending on the various situations, one will privilege this or that specific form of general inequality: colonial oppression, cultural appropriation, the primacy of white culture, the patriarchy, the conflicts of gender and so on.

There is a further paradox at work here: this struggle against inequality is self-destructive insofar as it undercuts its own foundation, and is thus unable to present itself as a project for positive global change:

> Precisely because the cultural heritage of the West cannot free itself from the inequalities that made its existence possible, past denouncers of inequality are themselves considered to benefit from one or another previously unrecognized inequality. [...] all the revolutionary movements and the notions of the revolution themselves are subject to suspicion now, simply because they belong to the long line of dead white males.

It is crucial to note that the new Right and the woke Left share this self-destructive stance. In late May 2023, the Davis School District north of Salt Lake City removed the Bible from its elementary and middle schools while keeping it in high schools after a committee reviewed the scripture in response to the Utah Parents United complaint, dated 11 December 2022, which said: 'You'll no doubt find that the Bible (under state law) has "no serious values for minors" because it's pornographic by our new definition.'[10] Is this just a case of Mormons against Christians? No; on 2 June 2023, a complaint was submitted about the signature scripture of the predominant faith in Utah, the Church of Jesus Christ of Latter-day Saints: district spokesperson Chris Williams confirmed that someone filed a review request for the Book of Mormon. Which political-ideological option is behind this demand? Is it the woke Left (exercising an ironic revenge against the Rightists banning courses and books on US history, Black Lives Matter, LGBT+, etc.), or is it the radicalized Right itself which (quite consequently) applied their criteria of family values to their own founding texts?

Ultimately it doesn't matter – what we should note is rather the fact that the same logic of prohibiting (or rewriting, at least) classic texts got hold of the new Right as well as the woke Left, confirming the justified suspicion that, in spite of their strong ideological animosity, they often formally proceed in the same way. In an act of cruel irony, the Western democratic tradition which usually praises itself for including self-criticism (democracy has flaws, but also includes striving to overcome its flaws ...), now brought this self-critical stance to its extreme – 'equality' is a mask of its opposite, etc., so that all that remains is the tendency towards self-destruction. But there is a difference between the Western anti-Western discourse and the anti-Western discourse coming from outside:

> while an anti-Western discourse is deployed within the West (and the West takes pride in this), another anti-western discourse is held outside of the West. Except that the first takes inequality for a fault, which one does not have the moral right to take advantage of; the second on the contrary sees in the inequality a virtue, on the condition that it is oriented in one's favor. Consequently, the proponents of the second anti-western discourse see the first as an indication of the enemy's decadence. They do not hide their contempt.

The woke radical reply to this is: the non-Western critics are right, the Western self-humiliation is fake, the non-Western critics are right to insist that whatever the West concedes to them, 'this is not that', we retain our superior frame and expect them to integrate – but why should they? The problem is, of course, that what the non-Western critics expect is, to put it brutally and directly, that the West renounces its way of life. The alternative here is: will, as the final result of the Western anti-Western critical stance, the West succeed in self-destroying itself (socially, economically) as a civilization, or will it succeed to combine self-defeating ideology with economic superiority? Milner is right: there is no big paradox in the fact that the self-denigrating critical mode is the best ideological stance for making sure there will be no revolutionary threat to the existing order.

However, one should supplement his claim with a renewal of the (fake, but nonetheless *actual*) revolutionary stance of the new populist Right: its entire rhetoric is based on the 'revolutionary' claim that the new elites (big corporations, academic and cultural elites, government services) should be destroyed, with violence if need be. In Varoufakis's terms, they propose a class war against our new feudal masters – the worst nightmare is here the possibility of a pact between the Western populist Right and the anti-Western authoritarians. It is easy to argue against the Trumpian ideology – never in the entire history of capitalism was the state more linked to corporate neo-feudal elites. But this is not nearly enough: the true task is not to squash the pseudo-revolutionary Trumpian energy but to redirect it towards its proper target, the techno-feudal masters.

What this means is that we should unconditionally resist any temptation to return to the state of things described by Milner, i.e., to re-assert cancelling and other similar ideological (and institutional) mechanisms. As I have already pointed out, Trumpian populism is a reaction to the liberal-democratic welfare state which approached its self-destruction (as well as its inability) through the focus on identity politics. The Trumpian pseudo-class-struggle is the return of the repressed of the Left-liberal identity politics. The task is thus clear: from the Left-liberal PC, we should take its broad goals, but without its bitter spirit of censoring and de facto logic of exclusion. Indeed, from the Trumpian populists, we should take their irreverent will to change. But what we should reject from both sides is a feature that found its clearest expression in Vance's notorious Munich speech on 14 February 2025 (quite correctly described as a masterpiece of 'terror on behalf of freedom').[11] Vance repeatedly questioned whether the US and Europe continue to share an agenda. He argued that the true threat to Europe stemmed not from external actors such as Russia or China but Europe's own internal retreat from some of its 'most fundamental values': 'What I worry about is the threat from within.' Among other things, Vance said:

> If you are afraid of the voices, the opinions and the conscience that guide your very own people ... If you're running in fear of your own voters, there is nothing America can do for you, nor for that matter is there anything you can do for the American people. [...] People dismissing voters' concerns, shutting down their media, protects nothing. It is the most surefire way to destroy democracy.[12]

The reality of this defence of freedom? In March 2025, the French government revealed that a researcher had been denied entry to the US after 'US authorities found messages about President Donald Trump on his phone.'[13] How does this crazy logic work? A unique incident that took place in Turkey back in 2011 offers a way into understanding it. The minister of the interior, Idris Naim Sahin, made a speech worthy of a very subtle dialectical speculation: he claimed that the Turkish police was imprisoning thousands of opposition members without evidence and without trial *to convince them that they were indeed free prior to their imprisonment.* In short, police put innocent people in prison to make clear to them that they were committing a pragmatic contradiction by simultaneously claiming, firstly, that there was no freedom in Turkey, and secondly, that they were imprisoned illegally (i.e., that their freedom had been taken from them). Here is a key passage from Sahin's speech:

> Freedom ... What freedom are you talking about when you complain about being imprisoned? If there's no freedom outside the prison, then the inside is no different. When you are complaining, it means there's a freedom outside. There's even a freedom to say 'I want to divide this country, freedom and autonomy does not suffice, I want to rebel', or whatever. You can't deny this. The only thing you deny to yourself is the freedom to talk about the freedoms you live in, because your head, your heart, your thought is mortgaged. You are not free to tell this. You don't have the freedom to tell that the freedoms you enjoy really exist. By destroying you as well as those who make you talk like that, we are trying to make you free, to save you from the separatists and their extensions. This is what we do. It is a very deep, very sophisticated job.[14]

The very absurdity and insanity of this argumentation is indicative of the 'mad' presuppositions of what one cannot but call liberal fascism at its extreme. Its first premise is a simple one: if you claim there is no freedom in our society, then don't protest when you are deprived of freedom, since you cannot be deprived of what you don't have. More interesting is the second premise: since the existing legal order is the order of freedom, those who rebel against it are effectively enslaved, unable to accept their freedom – they deprive themselves of the basic freedom to accept the social space of freedom. So when the police arrest you and 'destroy' you, they are basically setting you free, liberating you from your self-imposed enslavement. Arresting suspected rebels and torturing them thus becomes 'a very deep, very sophisticated job' with a metaphysical dignity.

Although this line of reasoning may appear to be based on a rather primitive sophism, it nonetheless contains a grain of truth: there effectively is no freedom outside the social order which, by way of limiting freedom, provides its space. But this grain of truth is the best argument against Sahin's sophism: precisely because the institutional limit to our freedom is the very form of our freedom, it matters how this limit is structured, what concrete form it takes. The trick of those in power – exemplified by Sahin's speech – is to present their form of this limit as the form of freedom as such, so that any struggle against them is the struggle against free society.

And is this not exactly how the prescribed freedom of Trump–Musk–Bezos (although Trump and Musk have split, they still share the same agenda) works? They present the form of freedom that they advocate as *the* definitive form of freedom, so that any critique can be presented as an attack on freedom as such – and the US as being fully justified in using all means necessary to defend itself against those who attack freedom, including causing them to lose their jobs, banning them from public spaces and even arresting them. Here we arrive back at Sahin's speech: those who claim that there is no freedom in Trump's US shouldn't protest when they are deprived of their freedom – fired, arrested or thrown out of the country – since you cannot be deprived of what you don't have.

Those who attack Trump (and Vance and Musk and ...) are, in their view, effectively self-enslaved by a false notion of freedom, so when Trump's administration moves against them, it is basically setting them free – it is freeing them from their self-imposed enslavement and thereby *forcing them to act as truly free*. What they are deprived of is only their 'freedom' to undermine the basics of the Western notion of freedom: in their fight against racism and sexism, they directly demand stronger state regulation even of our intimate spheres. *Les extremes se touchent*.[15] Should we really be surprised that Trumpians, the great opponents of cancel culture, come close to doing exactly the same things in a much more brutal way? Calling for the inclusion of freedoms, they end up ruthlessly excluding forms of freedom that do not fit their idea of liberty.

But do those in Europe who now advocate rearmament against the Russian threat as the only way to retain peace and freedom not commit a similar mistake? Does their logic – 'You want peace? Then rearm yourself so that others will not be tempted to attack you!' – not involve a similar paradox? Definitely not. In the same way that even a free market can only survive through strong state regulation which prevents monopolies arising, the sad truth is that peace has to be protected, often with arms. Freedom is here not enforced – quite the opposite; force is needed to defend freedom under threat.

Furthermore, the European call to rearmament is not only (and even not primarily) a move against the Russian threat; it is a move against the US. If Europe wants to establish itself as an autonomous sovereign force which will no longer have to rely on the US nuclear umbrella, it has to assert itself also as a strong military power. It is true that Europe is mired in complacent inertia: in contrast to the US and China, it has been slow to invest (in digitalization, in AI ...). However, I think that new military investments are not necessarily a step towards the 'fascistization' of Europe: they could also help to drag Europe out of its inertia and trigger its economic renaissance. Did the US not do exactly the same under Franklin Delano Roosevelt? The US only truly emerged from the Great Depression after 1940 and through military mobilization, so that in 1945 even non-military production was at its highest level, but one could hardly claim that Roosevelt was a fascist dictator. Today, Europe needs a Roosevelt-like mobilization for peace. And today's peaceniks come dangerously close to the American appeasers (who were vastly funded by Nazi Germany) pre-1942. The aggressor is always against militarization ... of its victim.

However, there is a problem with this European militarization. Radical as it may appear to be, it avoids confronting a crucial question: OK, Europe will get a strong united army, but *who will politically control this army, what political vision will sustain it*? How will this army function when the EU is less and less united, when some of its members (Hungary, Slovakia, Italy...) pursue a different global political agenda? Militarization will totally miss its goal without a clear political vision that justifies it. Without this vision, we will have a military behemoth without a clear purpose and thus open to all kinds of abuses.

Grab 'em by the Pussy

On 25 February 2025, Donald Trump posted a thirty-second video clip on his Truth Social account. The clip appeared to have been created with generative AI and was first put online by somebody with no connection to the White House. It shows the transformation of Gaza into a Gulf State-like resort, opening on footage of barefoot Palestinian children walking through Gazan rubble. After a title card asks 'What's next?', they walk towards a skyline of skyscrapers dominating Gaza's coast, and a voice sings: 'Donald's coming to set you free. Trump Gaza shining bright. Golden future, a brand-new light. Feast and dance. The deed is done.' The scenes shown are as follows: Teslas driving through the streets; someone with a striking resemblance to Elon Musk eating bread dipped in hummus; Hamas militants with full beards dancing flirtatiously in bikinis and sheer belly-dancing skirts; a child holding a giant, gold Trump balloon; Trump dancing with a scantily-clad woman in a nightclub; Musk showering people with cash; a 'Trump Gaza' building; golden Trump merch including his statues on sale; a gigantic golden Trump statue; Trump and Netanyahu lounging topless poolside while enjoying cocktails.[1] In whatever way one understands this clip, Palestinians are deprived of minimal dignity – and dignity is important to them, in spite of or rather because of their misery. On 20 October 2024, after a three-year-old Palestinian boy was killed by air-dropped aid in the southern city of Khan Younis in Gaza, his grandfather said: 'We don't want aid. We want dignity. Enough with the humiliation and insult that we are receiving from the Arabs, not just the Israelis.'[2]

It is easy to make fun of this weird clip, but it deserves a deeper analysis, even a consideration of its philosophical implications. Lacan claims that truth has the structure of a fiction – some traumatic or intense truths are more easily accepted if we present them as moves in a fictitious game. Say I am passionately in love but I am ashamed to declare it openly, so I use the situation where we play a pair of lovers in a theatre scene to express my love, knowing that it will not be attributed to me as a person. In today's political propaganda, the strategy is simpler: fiction has the structure of truth, i.e., a lie is presented as truth. The Trump–Gaza clip fits with neither of these two options. The first impression it gives us is, of course, that of a tasteless satire, of ridiculous irony – but when Trump himself posted it on Truth Social, it looks as if he appropriated it 'seriously', taking it as a probable vision of Gaza in the imminent future. Or was he aware that the clip was intended ironically and consciously decided to embrace his own caricature? The most probable version is that Trump didn't think about it much at all: he saw it is a funny crazy clip and said to himself, 'It will provoke controversy and make me even more popular, so why not?'

There are cases where the relationship between truth and fiction gets even more complex. In mid-February 2025, reports circulated that the Israeli military were dropping leaflets across the Gaza Strip which openly threatened the territory's entire population of more than two million people with forced displacement or/and death – here is the message:

> To the honorable people of Gaza,
> After the events that have taken place, the temporary ceasefire, and before the implementation of Trump's mandatory plan – which will impose forced displacement upon you whether you accept it or not – we have decided to make one final appeal to those who wish to receive aid in exchange for cooperating with us. We will not hesitate for a moment to provide assistance. Reconsider your position. The world map will not change if all the people of Gaza cease to exist. No one will feel for you, and no one will ask about you. You have been left alone to face your inevitable fate. Iran cannot even protect itself, let alone protect you, and you have seen with your own eyes what has happened. Neither America nor Europe care about Gaza in any way. Even your Arab countries, which are now our allies, provide us with money and weapons while sending you only shrouds. There is

little time left – the game is almost over. Whoever wishes to save themselves before it is too late, we are here, remaining until the end of time.

To add an obscene insult to injury, the message includes a passage from the *Quran*: 'We will certainly test you with a touch of fear and famine and loss of property, life, and crops. Give good news to those who patiently endure who say, when struck by a disaster, "Surely to Allah we belong and to Him we will all return."'[3] I don't think these leaflets (on the front of which there are photos of Netanyahu and Trump) were really dropped, but where did the story and the leaflet text originate? Not with the Palestinians but from unofficial Israeli sources as part of a complex campaign of psychological warfare.

The public diplomacy of Israel – called *'hasbara'* (roughly translated as 'explaining') – is a massive, well-coordinated effort to justify measures which are perceived as unacceptable by global opinion. This 'explaining' is done in multiple forms, by official state organs, private organizations and public figures (artists, journalists, scientists), but also as anonymous rumours spreading conspiracy theories or faked 'documents' attributed to the enemy. Another *hasbara* strategy is to allow (or solicit) lower-level political figures to state openly what the top leaders don't say openly or even deny – such statements, although not widely reported in the media, 'explain' what the more polite statements of top politicians imply. For example, Owen Jones has played on his podcast a recorded statement by the Israeli Deputy Parliament Speaker Nissim Vaturi which says: 'Who is innocent in Gaza? Civilians went out and slaughtered people in cold blood ... We need to separate women and children and kill the adults in Gaza, we are being too considerate.' And then he takes a step further, including even children: 'Every child born now – in this minute – is already a terrorist when he is born.'[4] This is in no way a mistake but part of a well-planned, complex strategy. With the amount of things to be explained away growing exponentially, the machinery of *hasbara* has had to rely on AI – so the Israeli government decided to use

AI-generated pro-Israel content and astroturfed social media campaigns. One of [these] new AI bots, which was reported in the press, was branded as FactFinder AI. It was designed to 'correct' misinformation, reconcile the paradoxes of *hasbara*, automate and expand *hasbara* campaigns, and reinforce Zionist narratives. However, when exposed to the real data landscape, the bot encountered undeniable realities – Israel's history of occupation, apartheid, and war crimes – and, instead of ignoring them (as Zionist *hasbara* does), the AI bot began processing them into responses. Israel's AI *hasbara* campaign backfired spectacularly, because even AI, when confronted with historical records, existing media narratives, and empirical data, could not fabricate a coherent pro-Israel stance because there is no coherent pro-Israel stance.[5]

The result of AI algorithms attempting to reconcile these conflicting directives and facts has been glitches that happen from time to time – glitches which are 'not just a technical malfunction; it is a symbolic rupture, an inevitable revelation of the inherent failure of Zionist ideology it was designed to serve.'[6] (Recall that in *The Matrix*, the glitches in what a subject sees – like the same cat appearing twice within seconds – also signal a glitch in the AI machine.) And what if the genocide leaflet is something similar: not simply a glitch but a second-level fake: a fake document whose very (rather obvious) 'glitches' (the leaflet is printed on a paper with Shin Bet marks; the reference to the Quran is ridiculous, no Muslim Arab would write like that ...) were intended and serve a precise function? What if the true goal of the 'discovery' of this leaflet was to sow doubt about its own authenticity, but at the same time leaving behind the vague impression that there must be some truth even in this fiction?

Such glitches have not yet attained the level of Trump-speak, which works in a different way: Trump doesn't even try to mask contradictions or constant shifts in his position. From day to day he blurts out what pops up in his mind – not (as some think) as part of his mental confusion but as the result of his (fully conscious) assumption of the role of a master beyond law and logic, one who asserts his power by way of demonstrating that he is not bound by the rules of political discourse. One day Zelensky is a legitimate leader of Ukraine to be received in the White House, the next day he is a dictator; one day Ukraine 'provoked' Russia, the next day Ukraine is merely defending itself against Russian aggression; one day the EU is a respected partner sorrowfully admonished for not doing enough for the West, the next the EU was formed to 'screw' the US . . .

A true master doesn't just obey rules and laws – from time to time, he makes an unexpected gesture, changes a political line, condemns or pardons a person, without giving any clear reasons. Such changes are a way for the master to assert his unconditional authority. When Stalin, usually late at night, would be confirming long lists of people to be shot, from time to time he would inexplicably cross out a name (although in all probability he didn't even know who the person was) – the total opacity of such acts made his authority unconditional. However, there is a difference between Stalin and Trump. What was with Stalin an exception to a brutal rule is for Trump a modus operandi. Trump is in this way effectively an anti-Stalin (not that this makes him any better – to paraphrase Stalin, Trump and Stalin are both worse). In both cases, factual truth takes second place; however, in Stalinism, the ignorance of factual truth is part of a precise hermeneutics – the very fact that a statement is factually not true delivers a clear message. The gap that separates exactitude (factual truth, accuracy about facts) and Truth (the Cause to which we are committed) was precisely formulated by Jean-Claude Milner:

> When one admits the radical difference between exactitude and truth, only one ethical maxim remains: never oppose the two. Never make of the inexact the privileged means of the effects of truth. Never transform these effects into by-products of the lie. Never make the real into an instrument of the conquest of reality. And I would allow myself to add: never make revolution into the lever of an absolute power.[7]

If the language of the new post-human AI will be a language of signals, no longer properly representing the subject, Stalinist language is its most fundamental antithesis. What characterizes human language, in contrast to the most complex signals exchanged by bees, is what Lacan called the 'empty speech', the speech whose denotative value (explicit content) is suspended on behalf of its functioning as an index of intersubjective relations between speaker and hearer. This suspension is the key feature of the Stalinist jargon. Here is a tragicomic detail that exemplifies this point: the public prosecutor in the show trial against the 'United Trotskyite-Zinovievite Centre' published a list of those that this 'Centre' was planning to assassinate (Stalin, Kirov, Zhdanov ...); to have one's name on this list became 'a bizarre honour since inclusion signified proximity to Stalin'.[8] Although Molotov was on good personal terms with Stalin, he was shocked to discover that he was not on the list: was this just a warning from Stalin, or an indication that soon it would be his turn to be arrested? (Indeed, a couple of years later his wife was arrested, accused of being an American and Jewish spy.) It was the Stalinist Soviet Union which was the true 'empire of signs'. In this sense, we may say that not only is Stalinism (also) a phenomenon of language, but that language itself is a Stalinist phenomenon – a certain key feature of human language finds its clearest expression in Stalinist jargon – only in human language can the statement 'I am not on the list of those to be assassinated by conspirators!' mean 'I am losing my political position!'

A story told by Soviet linguist Eric Han-Pira provides another perfect example of the Stalinist total semantic saturation of this 'empire of signs', the semantic saturation which, precisely, relies on the emptying of direct denotative meaning. For many years, when the Soviet media reported on the funeral arrangements of a member of the high nomenklatura, they would use a stock phrase: 'buried on Red Square by the Kremlin wall'. In the 1960s, however, because of the lack of space, most of the newly deceased dignitaries were cremated and urns with their ashes were placed in niches inside the wall itself – yet the same old cliché was used in press statements. This incongruity compelled fifteen members of the Russian Language Institute of the Soviet Academy of Sciences to write a letter to the Central Committee of the Communist Party, suggesting that the phrase be modified to fit the current reality: 'The urn with ashes was placed in the Kremlin wall.' Several weeks later, a representative of the Central Committee phoned the Institute, informing them that the Central Committee had discussed their suggestion and decided to keep the old formulation; he gave no reasons for this decision.[9]

According to the rules that regulated the Soviet 'empire of signs', the CC was right: the change would not be perceived as simply registering the fact that dignitaries are now cremated and their ashes placed in the wall itself; any deviation from the standard formula would be interpreted as a sign, triggering a frenzied interpretive activity. So, since there was no message to be delivered, why change things? One may oppose to this conclusion the possibility of a simple 'rational' solution: why not change the formulation and add an explanation that it means nothing, that it just registers a new reality? Such a 'rational' approach totally misses the logic of the Soviet 'empire of signs': since, in it, *everything* had some meaning, even and *especially* a denial of meaning, such a denial would trigger even more frantic interpretive activity – it would be read not only as a meaningful sign within a given, well-established, semiotic space, but as a much stronger meta-semantic indication that the very basic rules of this semiotic space were changing, thus causing total perplexity, panic even!

In Trump's discourse, language functions in a totally different way. Yes, he generates inconsistent statements again and again, but beneath them there is a clear 'general line' he follows, sustained by censorship of press and purges, much worse and more extensive than Cancel Culture, which almost remind us of Stalinism. Let us take a closer look at the press conference in the Oval Office of the White House which shocked the entire world, and let's focus on the details of manners, gestures and style, which may appear less important than the issues at stake but effectively disclose more about the underlying basic stance.[10]

The first thing that catches the eye is that we are watching two arrogant and self-assured US politicians treating the leader of Ukraine – who was under terrifying pressure, on the verge of a breakdown – in an extremely disrespectful and brutal way. The only country I know whose representatives resort to brutal language comparable to Trump's is Russia. The press representative of the Russian Ministry of Foreign Affairs, Marija Zaharova, wrote: 'How Trump and Vance held back from hitting that scumbag is a miracle of restraint.'[11] And, as expected, the chorus was joined by ex-president Medvedev who designated Zelensky a 'cocaine clown'. But such statements are made by the second-rank figures, never by the top leaders: at the level of public diplomacy, Trump and Vance violate the rules respected even by Hitler, Stalin and Mao. Only the North Korean state media occasionally resort to similar brutalities – no wonder Trump openly admires Kim Jong-Un as a good leader and sometimes calls him a friend.

Before Zelensky even entered the room, one of the White House personnel reproached him for showing disrespect by not being properly dressed. (Note that, like Churchill during World War II, Zelensky was in civilian fatigues since the beginning of the invasion – this was a political statement by him and not an accidental impoliteness.) Everything about Zelensky's treatment at the White House was disrespectful, and what makes it even worse was that Donald Trump, the man who set new standards for public vulgarity, shamelessly condemns others for behaving disrespectfully. The ultimate obscenity is to reproach someone for behaving disrespectfully in a form which is in itself an act of extreme disrespect. Mike Waltz described the way Zelensky reacted at the news that he was thrown out with a rather tasteless metaphor (also a misogynist dogwhistle): 'It's like a, you know, an ex-girlfriend that wants to argue, you know, everything that you said nine years ago, rather than moving the relationship forward.'[12]

So was the open conflict in the Oval Office a spontaneous outburst? The least one can say is that such an obscene display was laying dormant, just waiting to explode. We should bear in mind that, at the level of substantial content, *nothing new happened* – what took place is, to put it in Hegelian terms, a passage from '*An sich*' to '*Für sich*' (from 'in-itself' to 'for-itself'), from mere presence in the background to explicit positing of a content as such. However, this passage changes everything: once things are directly brought out, we find ourselves in a different space. Although everyone in a group might know very well something that is only 'in itself', it can still be interpreted away as a misunderstanding, as something we 'didn't really mean', but once it is directly said, it cannot be undone. In the case of the Oval Office meeting, this shift to 'for-itself' can be located precisely: although tensions were palpable all the time, the meeting became explicitly tense when Vance reproached Zelensky for not being sufficiently grateful for US help in Ukraine's war with Russia. Here is that part of the exchange:

VANCE: Just say thank you.

ZELENSKY: I said thank you – I say thank you to the American people.

TRUMP: You see, I think it's good for the American people to see what's going on. I think it's very important. That's why I kept this going so long. You have to be thankful. You don't have the cards. You're buried there. You people are dying. You're running low on soldiers. [...] Then you tell us, 'I don't want to cease fire.' If you could get a cease-fire right now, I tell you, you take it so the bullets stop flying and your men stop getting killed.

What followed was an open shouting match, unheard of in the domain of diplomacy where such a direct brutal exchange is supposed to happen behind closed doors – as some commentators noted, diplomacy died in the Oval Office. We – the public – witnessed something that one would expect to find at a negotiation among low-level mafia bosses.

J. D. Vance's argument – that, after years of trying to break Russia with arms, the time has come to try diplomacy – is so full of holes that it is fully transparent. War (Russian aggression) erupted after years of inefficient diplomatic attempts to find a solution – when Russia occupied Crimea back in 2014, diplomacy achieved nothing. The heroic Ukrainian resistance (sustained by Western help) didn't simply fail, it created conditions for possible negotiations; without this resistance, Ukraine would vanish as a state. Plus, as we have already seen, who are Trump and Vance to talk about diplomacy after breaking all the rules of diplomacy?

It is naive to claim that bringing the tensions out can clarify the situation. First, as we have already seen, bringing things out publicly can preclude possible solutions since it adds dimensions of aggression and humiliation to the situation which make it even more difficult to have a dialogue or resolve anything. Secondly, and more importantly, what happened in the Oval Office was *not* a cathartic purging, a healing process of letting out poisonous tension: the situation remained totally mystified, with Trump obviously mad at Ukraine and Europe plus Zelensky put in an impossible position – he had to defend Ukraine's vital interests, ignored by the US, while at the same time showing respect and gratitude since Ukraine's survival may depend on the US help.

Should we, then, blame Zelensky? Should he not have been more aware of the need for US help and acted in a more 'considerate' way (which means slavishly kowtowing to Trump)? The contrast with Macron, and especially with Starmer who, as Owen Jones put it, vanished up Trump's backside on his last visit to Washington, is clear and salutary.[13] I think Zelensky should not only not be reproached, but should be admired, his tragic predicament fully appreciated and empathized with: he defended himself clearly and counter-attacked, but he had to combine this with humiliating displays of respect for Trump who supports the Russian agenda. Trump's claim that Zelensky doesn't want a ceasefire but a continuous war was a lie, pure and simple: of course Zelensky wanted and continues to want peace, but – quite understandably – a peace which will be more than a ceasefire enabling a breathing space for Russia to reorganize and renew the attack. In short, he didn't want a Ukrainian version of the Gaza ceasefire which resulted in renewed pressure on the Palestinians to leave Gaza peacefully – i.e., to paraphrase Clausewitz's well-known definition of war as a continuation of politics by other means, such a ceasefire would be a continuation of war by peaceful means.

The day after condemning Russia for brutally bombing Ukraine, Trump changed his tune and said Putin was 'doing what anybody would do' when Russia launched a massive missile and drone strike on Ukraine days after the US cut off vital intelligence and military aid to Kyiv. Speaking to reporters in the Oval Office, Trump said he found it 'easier' to work with Russia than Ukraine and that Putin 'wanted to end the war'.[14] From Trump's standpoint, there was no contradiction here, he was just providing excuses in advance: if his efforts failed, it will be the fault of Ukraine which wants war while both Trump and Putin desire peace. The cards metaphor repeatedly used by Trump is also totally misleading – Zelensky was right to reply: 'I don't play cards.' The Jewish population of Nazi Germany also didn't hold any good cards, especially after 1938, but the contemporary governments and institutions who responded to their plight by effectively saying, 'Sorry, you don't have good cards – if you want us to fully support you, this could lead to a new world

war, so you're on your own' have been condemned by history ...
How can one argue against such logic? After the humiliating
requests to show more gratitude in the conversation, Zelensky put
out a brief post on X:

> Thank you America, thank you for your support, thank you for
> this visit. Thank you @POTUS, Congress, and the American
> people. Ukraine needs just and lasting peace, and we are working
> exactly for that.[15]

Was this almost compulsive repetition of 'thanks' meant to
demonstrate his gratitude for the lack of which he was criticized by
Trump and Vance, or is in this ridiculous message also an element
of irony, intended or not – like an Oscar-winning actor performing
the required genuflections in the direction of 'the industry'?

When Trump evokes humanitarian reasons, as he did with his
show of concern for Ukrainians dying in the war, there is always a
horror lurking behind his words. Remember that he also claimed
that Gaza should be emptied for humanitarian reasons, but neither
in the case of Gaza nor in the case of Ukraine did he raise the
obvious question: who is responsible for the destruction? Both in
Gaza and with Russia, 'America first' clearly means American
business first: US Secretary of State Marco Rubio extolled the
'extraordinary opportunities, economic and geopolitical, that the
United States and Russia could both seize once the war in Ukraine
was over'.[16] However, it is easy to see how this extolling of business is
not only an ideology in itself but also thoroughly permeated by
specific ideologico-political choices. Doing business in itself
presupposes a set of unwritten rules that are supposed to be
respected – as serious analysts know very well, business implies
basic *trust*. These rules are violated by Trump who thus turns
business into a brutal game of blackmail. As for political choices:
why treat China as the main enemy and dismiss any of the
'extraordinary opportunities' a collaboration with China may offer?
And, especially, why Trump's repeated characterization of Europe as
the main foe of the US, including the absurd claim that the EU was
created to 'screw' the US?[17] And there is also no need to point out
what Europe should do: if Trump claims that the EU was created to
screw the US, then OK, let's do it, fully, in all dimensions, politically,

economically and militarily. All options should be on the table, from a new alliance with China up to de-dollarization. In short, Europe should unite as much as possible and proclaim a state of emergency.

What Trump is doing in his obscene acts is applying to politics stances which he declared publicly years ago as a mere businessman and reality TV star. Recall a video clip from 2005 in which Trump describes his attempt to seduce a married woman and indicated he might start kissing a woman he was about to meet: 'I don't even wait. And when you're a star, they let you do it. You can do anything.... Grab 'em by the pussy. You can do anything.'[18] Recall, also, how in January 2015, during a meeting with a bipartisan group of senators at the White House, Trump referred to Haiti and some African nations as 'shithole countries'.[19] This is how one should describe the Oval Office fiasco in Trump's own terms: in view of the business opportunities offered by Russia, Ukraine is a shithole country, so let's grab Zelensky by his pussy – I am a political star and I can do whatever I want.

The horror of such acts reaches well beyond economic extortion and violating the rules of diplomacy. When a subject acts legally, his external acts do not violate any legal prohibitions and regulations; however, politeness (manners, gallantry, etc.) is more than just obeying external legality – it is the ambiguously imprecise domain of what one is not strictly obliged to do (if one doesn't do it, one doesn't break any laws), but what one is nonetheless expected to do. We are dealing here with implicit unspoken regulations, with questions of tact, with something towards which subjects have as a rule a non-reflected relationship: something that is part of our spontaneous sensitivity, a thick texture of customs and expectations which is part of our inherited substance of mores (what Hegel called *Sitten* and Lacan called the 'big Other'). Trumpian discourse (I use the term here not as jargon but in its strict Lacanian sense of a social link sustained by speech) thus poses a threat to the very substance of our social life, and directly contributes to the social disintegration observed by many analysts. The lack of manners simply excludes the other from communication: I pretend to listen to my partner, but I don't really hear him. Such a stance is becoming a mass phenomenon – here is what the Republican Senator Lindsay Graham said after the Oval Office event:

What I saw in the Oval Office was disrespectful, and I don't know if we could ever do business with Zelensky again. I think most Americans saw a guy that they would not want to go in business with, the way he handled the meeting.[20]

(Again, the term 'business' is very revealing here.) Graham then went on to urge Zelensky to prioritize a rare earth minerals deal over security guarantees or a ceasefire with Russia – an obscenity if there ever was one. The rare minerals deal was a clear case of brutal extortion by the US: you get our help (casually valued by Trump at 350 billion, which is definitely more than the actual sum) if you pay for it by allowing the US to exploit your natural resources for decades to come. Trump justified this deal with a weird line of argumentation: if the US were to provide direct military guarantees to Ukraine, this could lead to World War III; but if the US gets a strong economic interest in Ukraine, this fact alone could stop Russia engaging in further aggressive acts against Ukraine since such acts would seriously damage US interests ... the cynicism of this argumentation is breathtaking. What it amounts to is: it is not about freedom, it is about our economic interests – we will be exploiting Ukraine in any case, so you should allow us to do it in peace.

In other words, the proposed minerals deal was the price to be paid for security guarantees – the minerals deal without security guarantees is, for the Ukrainian side, totally meaningless. The whole affair gets even more offensive if we combine it with Trump's and Vance's requests for gratitude: not only does Ukraine have to perform slavish displays of public gratitude for US help, it then *has to pay for it*. No wonder we didn't have to wait long for a reaction to Graham's turn against Zelensky from none other than Tucker Carlson, the public commentator who personifies the link between Trump and Putin (recall his ultra-benevolent interview with Putin):

> One of the most striking things about yesterday's Zelensky press conference was Lindsey Graham's reaction to it. The two are old friends, but Graham disavowed him within the hour. This was more than just transactional disloyalty. It was scapegoating. Lindsey Graham knows what's coming. Over the past three

years, with the tacit support of its western patrons, the Ukrainian government has committed a remarkable number of serious crimes. The Ukrainians sold huge quantities of American weapons on the international black market at twenty cents on the dollar. These weapons are now in the hands of armed groups around the world, including Hamas, the Mexican drug cartels and the forces now controlling Syria. God knows what the Ukrainians have done with the pathogens in American biolabs in their country. Even US intel agencies aren't sure. The Ukrainians have also murdered a number of people in various countries in political assassinations, and tried to murder others, including American journalists and a European head of state. This is all true, and it's all going to come out at some point. Better to start blaming it on Zelensky now.[21]

A case of political 'realism' if ever there was one. Trump and his gang like to present themselves as 'realists', inheritors of the legacy of Henry Kissinger, repeating all the time the mantra that they just want to prevent concrete suffering, destruction and the deaths of ordinary people. However, as John Ganz perspicuously pointed out, what such a 'realist' view discounts is precisely the concrete suffering of hundreds of thousands of individuals:

> we are not seeing a sovereign nation invaded, its cities destroyed, we are not seeing children being burned, instead we are seeing a 'proxy war' or 'a great power struggle.' To focus on what we are actually seeing makes us dangerous sentimentalists, but to see the great forces behind all of it, that makes us good, hard-headed 'realists.' In its capacity to transform reality, cynicism is apparently much more potent ideological agent in our era than fanatical belief in great causes.[22]

Zelensky warned Vance of the seriousness of the Russian threat: 'you have [a] nice ocean and don't feel now, but you will feel it in the future.' Trump immediately jumped in: 'Don't tell us what we're going to feel!'[23] Trump's arrogance seduced him into clearly misreading Zelensky: his 'you will feel it' had nothing to do with subjective experiencing, but meant that the US will be impacted by political and military pressure, while Trump typically read it as

Zelensky ordering him how to feel – if anyone was trying to dictate the emotional responses of others, it was Trump and Vance who were ordering Zelensky to feel gratitude... In a situation that befits a normal exchange between allies, Zelensky should have answered: it is Ukraine which deserves respect and gratitude for engaging in a brutal war to defend not only its own sovereignty but also to protect the freedom of all of Europe and ultimately of the US themselves.

13 Why Evil Men Need Noble Spirits

Kafka's short story from 1912, 'The Judgement' ('Das Urteil', which could also be translated as 'The Verdict'), is today closer to reality than ever. The story is the portrait of a weak father who drives the subject to suicide, and it's worth recapping the plot briefly: George, a young merchant, sits in his room writing to 'a friend from his youth', who some years ago left for Russia to set up a business that is now failing.[1] George's letter has finally revealed something has been postponing telling his friend – that he is engaged to marry Frieda, 'a young woman from a prosperous family'. George goes to check on his father, with whom he has lived since his mother died two years ago, and is struck by the darkness of his father's room and the stature the older man still possesses:

> 'Ah, George,' said his father, coming up at once to meet him. His heavy night shirt opened up as he moved and the ends of it flapped around him. 'My father is still a giant,' said George to himself.

When George informs his father that he has just written a letter to his friend, updating him on his upcoming marriage, his father questions the very existence of the friend in Russia and accuses George of deceiving him about the happenings of the business. George insists on having his father lie down in bed for a while, carrying him to the bed in his arms, but the father claims his son wants him dead: 'You wanted to cover me up – I know that, my little offspring – but I am not yet under the covers.' Moreover, he admits to knowing his son's friend, and, in fact, to having been carrying on a correspondence with him concurrently with George's. He claims to have swayed the friend's loyalty from George to himself, and that the friend reads the father's letters while disposing of George's without reading them. He makes George feel terrible, suggesting that George has ignored his friend ever since he moved away to Russia.

George stood in a corner, as far away as possible from his father. A long time before he had firmly decided to observe everything closely, so he would not be surprised somehow by any devious attack, from behind or from above. Now he recalled again this long-forgotten decision and forgot it, like someone pulling a short thread through the eye of a needle.

The father does not appreciate George's love and care, maintaining he can take care of himself. As George shrinks back, terrified, the father accuses him of being selfish, judges and sentences him: 'Essentially you've been an innocent child, but even more essentially you've been a devilish human being! And therefore understand this: I sentence you now to death by drowning!' George '[feels] himself hounded from the room'; he runs from his home to a bridge over a stretch of water, swings himself over the railing and plunges, apparently to his death. His last words are: 'Dear parents, I have always loved you nonetheless.'[2]

In an hour-long speech at the UN General Assembly on 23 September, Trump unleashed an extraordinary tirade which sounds like the explosive vituperations of George's father. Britain and Europe are 'going to hell' because of immigration, climate change is 'the greatest con job ever perpetrated on the world' and a culture war with Europe was openly declared.[3] This speech was one big recitation of crimes and condemnation to death, exactly like George's overblown father who condemns his son to suicide. And, as in Kafka's story, Europe is running to a bridge to kill itself off as the united global power it should be.

One should also note that in spite of his pro-Ukrainian turn, Trump and Putin both oppose the European multicultural and pro LGBT+ stance. Although he advised Europe to help Ukraine regain all its territory and to bomb Russian planes and drones if they enter the NATO territory, he didn't say the US will help Europe. It is clear what his aim was: in the case of a direct Europe–Russia war, Trump will again play the role of the dominant peacekeeper and negotiate an armistice ...

An extraordinary social and psychological change is taking place right in front of our eyes, a change whose logic was described a century ago by Henri Bergson in his *The Two Sources of Morality and Religion*. In a passage that's often quoted, including by me, Bergson describes how on 4 August 1914, when war was declared between France and Germany, he experienced a strange 'feeling of admiration for the facility of the passage from the abstract to the concrete: who would have thought that such a formidable event can emerge in reality with so little fuss?'[4] Crucial here is the modality of the break between before and after: before its outburst, the war appeared to Bergson '*simultaneously probable and impossible*: a complex and contradictory notion which persisted to the end';[5] after its outburst, it all of a sudden become real *and* possible, and the paradox resides in this retroactive appearance of probability:

> I never pretended that one can insert reality into the past and thus work backwards in time. However, one can without any doubt insert there the possible, or, rather, at every moment, the possible insert itself there. Insofar as unpredictable and new reality creates itself, its image reflects itself behind itself in the indefinite past: this new reality finds itself all the time having been possible; but it is only at the precise moment of its actual emergence that it *begins to always have been*, and this is why I say that its possibility, which does not precede its reality, will have preceded it once this reality emerges.[6]

An event is thus experienced first as impossible but not real (the prospect of a forthcoming catastrophe which, however probable we know it is, we nevertheless do not believe it will really happen and thus dismiss it as impossible), and then as real but no longer impossible (once the catastrophe occurs, it is 'renormalized', perceived as part of the normal run of things, as always-already having been possible). The gap which makes these paradoxes possible is the one between knowledge and belief: we *know* the (ecological) catastrophe is possible, probable even, yet we do not *believe* it will really happen. And is this not what is happening today, right in front of our eyes? A decade ago, a public debate on torture or the participation of neo-fascist parties in a western

European democratic government was dismissed as an ethical catastrophe which was impossible, which 'really cannot happen'; once it happened, we immediately got accustomed to it, accepting it as obvious, as inevitable, of course it was always going to be this way ... What I am afraid of is that, if a larger military conflict breaks out between Russia and NATO countries, it will obey the same logic. Now we talk about it without really believing this war can happen; once it erupts (if it does), I predict we will simply get used to it.

But the central shift happening now is the rise of new populist nationalism in so-called Western democracies. This is taking place not only in the US (Trump), France (le Pen) or Italy (Meloni), but in the UK, which is the key country in this ongoing shift at the time of writing. I think the phenomenon described by its partisans as 'the awakening of the people' is largely the result of the utter failure of the 'moderate' centre or Left. Anti-immigrant populists shamelessly circulate non-verified stories about rapes and other crimes of the refugees in order to give credibility to their claim that immigrants pose a threat to our way of life. However, all too often multicultural liberals proceed in a similar way: they pass in silence over actual differences in the 'ways of life' between refugees and Europeans since mentioning them may be seen to promote Eurocentrism. Recall the case of Rotherham in the UK where, a decade or so ago, police discovered that a gang of Pakistani youth was systematically raping over a thousand poor white young girls – the data were ignored or downplayed in order not to trigger Islamophobia ...

Or recall the murder of Iryna Zarutska, a twenty-three-year-old Ukrainian refugee, on a local train in Charlotte (North Carolina) in early September 2025. The video that covered that part of the train shows Iryna get on the light rail at the East West Boulevard station stop and take a seat directly in front of Decarlos Brown, the suspect. At first, nothing seems unusual, other than Brown appearing upset in his seat – nothing that could cause a commotion. Just four minutes later, Brown is seen pulling out what appears to be a pocket knife and suddenly stabbing Zarutska deep into the throat multiple times. She collapses as Brown calmly walks to the front of the car, takes off his sweater and wraps his bloodied hand in it before exiting the train. Other passengers were alerted to what happened after seeing a trail of blood and Zarutska collapsed – but (for me, at least) the most depressing fact is that, after the act of killing, there is also no commotion: the (mostly Black) passengers sitting nearby do nothing, they just sit and stare, embarrassed.[7] The murder was, as expected, widely commented upon and decried by the new Right commentators from Kirk to Trump himself who were mostly playing a racial card: a convicted Black criminal killed a white girl ... However, instead of providing a serious interpretation, the liberal Left mostly downplayed the event because it didn't fit the politically correct co-ordinates.

Charlie Kirk was right to focus on this murder – he didn't just play the race card but detected where the true horror resided. That's why Kirk should absolutely not be reduced to a Rightist fanatic – yes, we have to reject his racist and sexist views, but he remains a much more ambiguous figure. The first important feature is the form of his public activity: polite and patient argumentation without any brutal and humiliating excesses. As to the content of his acts, Slovene commentator Mojca Pišek went so far as to call him a 'socialist reformer'[8] – he was not there yet, but he was clearly moving in this direction. In the last year of his activity, he gradually moved from the standard Rightist populism to a greater sensitivity about what we cannot but call class struggle: how big corporations and the 'deep state' (with the support of the academy and public media) rule unencumbered over the mass of ordinary people, even (or especially) when they play the game of woke-ish cancel culture. The crucial thing is that Kirk doesn't regress to conspiracy theories: to put it bluntly, he more and more sees the problem in the system itself. In this tendency, he is close to Curtis Yarvin, who also should not be dismissed as a techno-Trumpian. Yarvin's scathing description of our 'liberal democracies' as barely concealed forms of oligarchy, including his point that actual democracy would be even worse and more dangerous, should be an obligatory reading for every serious Leftist.[9] Both Kirk and Yarvin remain vaguely Trumpian, but for an understandable reason: they clearly perceive Trump as someone who disturbed the system and thus opened up a path of radical change.

It is precisely their Trumpian starting point which enables Kirk and Yarvin to approach or formulate some basic Leftist insights without falling prey to the politically correct mess that prevents today's Left from formulating a serious alternate vision. To get rid of the self-sabotaging layer of today's Left, one has to go through their apparently most radical opponents – Bernie Sanders himself gives hints in this direction. Here is what none other than Steve Bannon said a couple of months ago:

> The Trump administration will use its legal powers to bust up the monopolistic power of Big Tech. We're going to break up Facebook. We're going to break up Google. We're going to break up Amazon. We're going to break ... I think hopefully we get to eventually break up Walmart. You've got too much concentration of private power.[10]

Recall how during Trump's first term Bannon was thrown out of the White House because he advocated much higher taxes for the rich (from 25 per cent to 40 per cent)!

I wrote years ago that the reason liberals are obsessed with Trump is because they have elevated him into a fetish: Trump is the last thing the liberals see before they would have to confront the spectre of class struggle, and their gaze is fixated on him in order not to see what is behind him. So how do we see what lies behind? By focusing on the antagonism that pervades the Trumpian field. As is well known, the Trumpians are vaguely divided into populists (Bannon) and technocrats (Yarvin): the tension between them seems irreducible since you cannot simultaneously advocate corporate digitalization of our lives and the local assemblies of ordinary people. My crazy hypothesis is that only a new Left can bring together these two aspects (techno-Trumpians and populist Trumpians) in the guise of digitalization under popular control.

Yes, the symbolic mechanisms of how the new digital Right is seducing millions are well known and have been described in detail. However, in cases like that of Charlie Kirk's murder, something more is at stake – nothing less than a redefinition of (the ideological self-perception of) a nation. This redefinition does not only have international implications, but can find expression also in brutal violence against minor features of the behaviour of special groups. In Poland, media outlets are raising alarms about a new viral trend among the younger generation called 'Szon Patrol'. 'Szon' in Polish means 'slut'. The name 'Szon Patrol' is mainly adopted by males who roam the streets in fluorescent vests to harass and publicly judge girls and women through hateful and moralistic speeches; a self-appointed 'slut patrol'. This trend started during school vacations and has already amassed over 12,000 videos related to these patrols.[11]

On a much more massive level, there is the mega-concert organized by nationalist, Catholic Croat singer Marko Perković (better known as Thompson) at a hippodrome in Zagreb on 5 July 2025. Around 500,000 tickets were sold in advance, making it the biggest concert where the public has to buy tickets in the history of humanity (or so the organizers claim). So who is Perković? Born in 1966, in 1991 he joined the Croatian forces fighting Serb aggression and used the American Thompson gun during his time in the war, which became his nickname and later, his stage name. So yes, Perković is a man of culture – however, to paraphrase Joseph Goebbels, his motto is: 'When I hear the world culture, I reach for my Thompson.'

The lyrics of his songs often feature patriotic sentiments and relate to religion, family, the Croatian War of Independence, politics and media, but also contain notorious positive references to the Ustaša regime during World War II and their war crimes which were too brutal even for the Nazis. Accused of neo-Nazism in 2004, he is prohibited from performing in many Western states. Some of his fans are known for their ultranationalism, demonstrated by Ustaša uniforms (including black hats associated with the movement), symbols, and banners. At the beginning of his mega-hit 'Bojna Čavoglave', Perković invokes *'Za dom – spremni!*' (*'For home [land] – ready!'*), the Ustaša military salute. One has to admit that the setting of this song relies on a masterful practice of, again, what Hegel would have called 'concrete universality': there is no mention of big military events, just a couple of young men defending a small Croat village in southern Bosnia from a Serb attack. In 2015, Perković performed in Knin in front of some 80,000 spectators for the twentieth anniversary celebration of the Croatian military's Operation Storm with many of those in attendance singing pro-Ustaša songs and chanting slogans such as 'Kill a Serb' and 'Here we go Ustaša'.[12]

However, we totally misread this situation if we read it as an expression of nostalgia for a Fascist past: even if it may appear like that, we are getting here the properly utopian vision of an imagined *future*, the vision of a community which holds out the promise that we can immerse ourselves in it and leave behind our alienation and isolation. One should never forget that the majority of Thompson's fans are young men of around twenty – without irony, one should say that they are failed Communists. More precisely, what characterizes the figure of Thompson is a tension between his explicit public image – not an Ustaša-Fascist, just a modest Catholic nationalist ready to defend his homeland – and a complex subtext permeated by clear and all-pervasive Ustaša signs and clues. Thompson is not lying when he repeatedly insists: 'I am not an Ustaša, just a patriot.' However, in some sense this makes things even worse: if he were to declare himself openly as Ustaša, this would limit his appeal; what he achieves through the way he functions is that *the very idea of being a patriot is appropriated by the neo-Fascist discourse*. Consequently, if you attack him for his Fascism, he can quickly reply that you are a pro-Serb traitor to Croatia.

Thompson thrives in this in-between state, acceptable both to the established Right and to neo-Fascists – no wonder even Pope Benedict XVI granted him an audience in December 2009. Typically, top Croatian politicians did not attend his big Zagreb concert, but Prime Minister Plenković attended the general rehearsal a day before with his sons and was greeted personally by Thompson ... Apropos Thompson, we should paraphrase Gideon Levy's comments on the hegemonic role of Ben-Gvir and Smotrich in Israel: 'The problem lies not only with the two extremist ministers, but with Israeli society as a whole, including those who consider themselves moderates. Do you understand now, diplomats and decision-makers? In Israel, we are all Ben-Gvir and Smotrich.'[13] The problem lies not only with Thompson as an extremist singer, but with Croat society as a whole, including those who consider themselves moderates. Do you understand now, diplomats and decision-makers? In Croatia, we are all Thompson.

This logic of 'we are all ...' does not mean that we all become fanatical believers: it includes its apparent opposite, a brutal irony which is even worse than direct brutality. In September 2025 we learned that a controversial new trend on TikTok has sparked outrage as Israeli content creators mock the ongoing conflict in Gaza. In the viral videos, young creators pose as members of a fictional humanitarian organization, calling family and friends to solicit donations for Palestinian children. The callers then film the often heated reactions, which typically involve angry shouting and swearing, before revealing that it's all part of a prank.[14]

Maybe these shameless pranksters are even worse than fanatical perpetrators of genocide.

One usually treats belief in God as the most intimate question – some friends sometimes ask me: 'I know this is improper to ask you, it probes too much into your intimacy, but do you believe in God?' Out of politeness I don't give them what my true answer would be: you are wrong, your question is wrong, there is nothing intimate in believing in God, your belief is basically external, materialized in your acts and interactions with others. A typical believer doesn't believe him/herself, he believes there is some kind of Other who is supposed to believe, and belief is primarily a belief in such an Other. This is what Lacan aims at with his notion of 'big Other': not an omnipotent god but a space or level of discourse whose functioning presupposes God. You yourself can be as cynical and manipulative as you want, but precisely as such you continue to rely on a big Other who believes in your place, instead of you. That's why the true formula of atheism is not 'I don't believe in God' but 'there is no big Other (who believes in God)'. As Chesterton put it more than a century ago, all religions accept that there are people who don't believe in God, but it's only in Christianity that God (on the Cross) doesn't believe in himself.

Thompson, therefore, is much more than just a musical or cultural event, he is a phenomenon that is now inscribed into the very core of the Croat identity. To use Gramsci's terms, he is the latest winner in the struggle for ideological hegemony in Croatia: to assert yourself as a Croat, you *have* to take a stance towards him – just to ignore him means tolerating him ... And the same holds for the gigantic anti-immigrant demonstration in the UK on Saturday, 13 September 2025: 110,000 anti-immigrant demonstrators protested in central

London under the slogan 'unite our kingdom', and millions joined them in other big cities. Elon Musk addressed the crowd via video link and issued nothing less than a call for revolution: he said a 'dissolution of parliament' and a 'change of government' was needed in the UK, and also railed against the 'woke mind virus'. Other speakers included Katie Hopkins and French far-right politician Éric Zemmour (in the past supported by Putin).[15] What we were witnessing there was an attempted '(re)awakening' of what being British means, leaving behind the sleepy Great Britain resigned to its decay, tolerating its multicultural space in which being English is just one of the particular facets. This motif of awakening to one's true identity was omnipresent in Nazi Germany whose slogan was '*Deutschland, erwache!*', as well as in the late 1980s in Serbia under Milošević – this motif of awakening, of course, amounted to its exact opposite: a call to immerse yourself in your national ideology, to surrender your powers of thought and critique and judgement to it.

We are not dealing with political parties here but with much more fundamental social movements which aim to permeate the entire social body in its economic, political and ideological aspects. Repulsive as they are, these movements are based on the correct insight that the standard liberal multi-party politics is becoming irrelevant, that it is more and more unable to catch the spirit that moves the crowds of population. (Again, Curtis Yarvin did a good job in presenting this decay of democracy which is not a recent phenomenon but is inscribed into its very notion.) This is why we shouldn't be surprised that the latest awakening-protest occurred in the UK, a country in which the traditional ruling parties (first the Conservatives, then the Labour party) are falling apart and the government is more and more perceived as irrelevant and impotent, unable to preserve the sovereignty of a nation. It is also important to note that the protesters effectively demanded a kind of revolution: using his prerogatives (which are usually a mere formality), the king should dissolve the parliament . . . And what then? There are now in the UK only two authentic political parties with the true power to mobilize, one already existing (Nigel Farage's Reform UK) and the other not yet formally existing (Jeremy Corbyn's and Zarah Sultana's Our Party) – unfortunately, as befits the Left, this party got caught in a split even before it was formally constituted. Will this new party (although it has a vast reservoir of voters) succeed in truly mobilizing voters? With what motifs? Anti-genocide struggle or anti-racist struggle are definitely not enough, so one can safely predict that in these ideal elections Reform UK would win.

We often hear that the Left should oppose to the Rightist politics of fear (targeted against immigrants, LGBT+, etc.), some positive vision of a new society. However, my perception is the opposite one: Trumpian populism denies the big threats to our very survival (ecological crisis, the growth of AI ...), i.e., it attacks people who claim our lives are under threat – to paraphrase a statement made famous by Roosevelt, Trump's claim is that the only thing we have to fear is fear itself (spread by the enemies of our societies). If it is to have any chance, the Left should focus on these threats and insist that we have to prepare for a global catastrophe – the new Communism will be a war Communism. And it is for this very reason that the Left has many things to learn from figures like Kirk. At Kirk's memorial service in Arizona on 21 September 2025, his widow forgave his killer – but Trump did not, characterizing Kirk as 'a missionary with a noble spirit and a great, great purpose' and going on to say:

> He did not hate his opponents. He wanted the best for them. That's where I disagreed with Charlie. I hate my opponents. And I don't want the best for them.[16]

This apparent inconsistency is a key feature of the Trumpian universe. Trump is, of course, not a 'noble spirit': he hates his opponents and considers them trash, to be swept aside, annihilated. However, in order to somehow justify his brutal hatred, he needs a figure like Kirk as a good man who wants the best also for his enemies. (It's a little bit like Christians who need the good Christ because his death justifies brutal persecution of anti-Christians.) This is why Kirk needs to be elevated into a figure of a martyr of almost divine proportions: this elevation is just the obverse of the Trumpian brutality. The standard hypocritical logic claims that we are attacking a country of a people to help the victims of its oppressive regime. In the 1930s, even Japan argued that it occupied most of China to civilize its people – that the Chinese people were like naughty children who had to be disciplined for their own good ... In the ongoing Middle East war, Bernard-Henri Levy has tried to follow this line: Israel is doing what it does in Gaza and on the West Bank to help Palestinians, to liberate them from the grip of Muslim fundamentalists who oppress them ...

However, it is not enough to reverse this stance and accomplish acts which we expect to produce good consequences for all affected by them. The logic gets here more complex – recall how Walter Benjamin brutally rejected Goethe's guiding principle, 'Try to ensure that everything in life has a consequence.' Benjamin's scathing comment:

This is without doubt one of the most detestable of maxims, one that you would not expect to run across in Goethe. It is the imperative of progress in its most dubious form. It is not the case that the consequence leads to what is fruitful in right action, and even less that the consequence is its fruit. On the contrary, bearing fruit is the mark of evil acts. The acts of good people have no 'consequence' that could be ascribed (or ascribed exclusively) to them. The fruits of an act are, as is right and proper, internal to it. To enter into the interior of a mode of action is the way to test its fruitfulness.[17]

There is an obvious counter-argument: what about acting to prevent global warming, or nuclear war, or the domination of AI? In this cases, aren't consequences the only things that matter at all? And doesn't this imply that Benjamin's argumentation relies on the old distinction between *poiesis* and *praxis*? 'Poiesis' is an activity which aims at producing a product that will exist after the activity is performed (making a work of art, a table, or whatsoever), while 'praxis' is an activity which is its own goal (like performing a work of art). However, one can argue that activities which aim at an external goal also have an immanent value. Imagine a big collective act to construct something that would diminish environmental damage: even if it fails, this activity actualizes a form of social solidarity and thus displays an immanent positive value. So what bears the mark of evil is the very exclusive orientation on an external goal (bad or good) which ignores 'the interior of [the] mode of action'.

Jean-Claude Milner has pointed out that for non-European countries, war is a normal state of things, always lurking in the background, and the times of peace are just occasional pauses between armed conflicts, while in the Christian West, peace is considered as the big culmination of historical progress, as the final state towards which we all strive.[18] Nowhere is this clearer than in Nazi Germany, where the state evoked all the time the *'ewiger Frieden'* (eternal peace) which would come to pass after the final victory, thus mandating and justifying total mobilization for the last war to end all wars. Today, the same madness is spreading around the world: Trump brought peace by fully supporting Israel and bombing Iran, Netanyahu tries to bring peace in the Middle East by expanding the war against Palestinians and engaging in genocide (which is in a way quite appropriate: after you annihilate your enemies, there *is* peace ...). So there is some logic in the crazy fact that both Trump and Netanyahu are proposed by some states as candidates for the Nobel Peace Prize ... At its extreme, cancel culture proceeds in a similar way: it fights for tolerance and diversity by brutally excluding all those who contest its own definition of tolerance and diversity.

Three conclusions are to be drawn from this situation. First, maybe learning to live with a threat of war is the only way to bring peace. Second, beware of 'noble spirits' whose function is to justify brutality. Third, in a truly emancipated society, people do not engage in acts which have good consequences – they engage in acts which have no consequences.

Donald Trump as a Gramscian

To account for our complex situation, (not only) Leftists refer to Antonio Gramsci's remark from his *Prison Notebooks*: "The crisis consists precisely in the fact that the old is dying and the new cannot be born; in this interregnum a great variety of morbid symptoms [*fenomeni morbosi*] appear."[1] In terms of social change, capitalism is disintegrating but the new socialist order cannot be born and we get morbid symptoms (like techno-feudalism); in the sexual economy the old patriarchy is disintegrating and the new free sexuality cannot be born, so we are getting morbid symptoms, etc. The worst illusion is that a direct smooth passage from the Old to the New is possible and that we simply missed taking it due to our contingent limitations – for example, the illusion that Stalinism arose because the first revolution happened in a wrong place, in 'backwards' Russia and not in the developed West.

In view of the recent worldwide rise of fascisms as the reaction to the crisis of global capitalism, Todd McGowan has suggested that we should reverse another well-known line of Walter Benjamin's: 'It's not that every fascism is the result of a failed revolution but that fascism is the natural response that capitalism engenders.'[2] Capitalism reacts to a crisis with some form of fascism, and the emancipatory resistance is a reaction to this fascist threat – in short, no Mamdani without Trump. So what if we turn things on their head? Perhaps the true 'morbid symptom' is our image of the proper New that we expected to emerge, and the solution is precisely and only to be sought in the desperate improvisations by means of which we try to avoid the catastrophe at the horizon.

Only against this background can we account for the fact that Gramsci is a key point of reference of the new populist Right. Trump and his cohorts are the true 'cultural Marxists', directly appropriating (their version of) struggle for ideological hegemony as it was conceptualized by Antonio Gramsci: struggle for hegemony means that the actual constellation of social forces is not directly reflected in ideological space. Opposing social forces struggle to appropriate into their ideological project elements of shared popular tradition (national history, religion and morality, etc.), and the winner is the one who succeeds in presenting its ideological project as 'universal', as encompassing most of the moments that constitute a social identity of a people. Trumpian populism thus unites in its project elements of working-class resistance to big corporate capital with affirmation of the 'creative' spirit of capitalism and the hatred of foreigners as the disturbing element in the social body. (Let's not forget Gramsci developed his notion of hegemony as a reaction to the victory of Fascism in Italy.)

The way the new populist Right is using concepts taken from the tradition of great progressive theory reached its peak with Peter Thiel and J. D. Vance appropriating the theories of Rene Girard, especially his notions of mimetic desire and sacrifice. Decades ago, Thiel was literally a student of Girard, and Girard's notion of mimetic desire gave him the idea for using digital media to expand ideas and thus control public opinion; later, he also made Vance read Girard. Even the notion of sacrifice has been mobilized in a distorted way: while Girard wants to break out of the closed circle of sacrificial logic, Thiel and Vance use it to conceptualize the exclusion of immigrants, sexual minorities, etc.[3] Here are two further examples of the new Right's struggle for hegemony. Gideon Levy recently wrote in *Haaretz*:

> According to opinion polls, the majority of Israelis support these massacres and even anticipate the implementation of the population transfer plan that may follow them. Therefore, international pressure and sanctions must target Israel as a whole, without exception. The problem lies not only with the two extremist ministers, but with Israeli society as a whole, including those who consider themselves moderates. Do you understand now, diplomats and decision-makers? In Israel, we are all Ben-Gvir and Smotrich.[4]

Here the position of enunciation matters: *only an Israeli Jew* can and should say this – if said from outside, it would come close to anti-Semitism. Is the success of radical aggressive Zionism not also a supreme case of the struggle for hegemony, a particular stance which was for a long time marginalized succeeding in dominating the entire field ('we are all Ben-Gvir and Smotrich')? So how does the populism do it? The key strategy is here what Katherine Dee called visualization as a magical practice:

> You create a detailed mental image and hold it, return to it, feed it with emotion and repetition until it becomes more real than physical reality itself. Your brain starts filtering the world through this image. You notice every piece of evidence that confirms it and dismiss what doesn't. You've reprogrammed your perception. The basic idea is the same: our focused intentions somehow influence reality in ways science can't explain. It works in both directions, positive and negative. The most dangerous curse is making someone believe they're cursed. It's especially effective on the internet – where magic seems to become real. When thousands simultaneously focus negative attention on someone, each person becomes primed to see that individual negatively. They feel permitted – even encouraged – to attack. The hex becomes self-fulfilling through thousands of small actions: unfollows, harsh comments, cancelled invitations, hostile interpretations. And in the darkest cases, it creates an atmosphere where violence becomes more thinkable – where someone already on the edge might feel the collective 'permission' to act.[5]

Not only are the origins of these concepts Leftist, but the Left also regularly uses them. Just recall the clips showing how, on 25 May 2020,

> George Floyd, a 46-year-old Black American man, was murdered in Minneapolis by Derek Chauvin, a 44-year-old White police officer. Chauvin knelt on Floyd's neck for over nine minutes while Floyd was handcuffed and lying face-down in the street. Two other police officers, J. Alexander Kueng and Thomas Lane, assisted Chauvin in restraining Floyd. Lane had also pointed a gun at Floyd's head before he was handcuffed. A fourth

officer, Tou Thao, prevented bystanders from intervening ... After several minutes, Floyd stopped speaking. For the last few minutes, he lay motionless, and Kueng found no pulse when urged to check. Chauvin ignored bystanders' pleas to lift his knee from Floyd's neck ...[6]

These endlessly repeated clips affected the viewers precisely in the way described by Dee.

Recall as well the photo of the bodies of Oscar Ramirez and his daughter Valeria from 2019.

The grim reality of the migration crisis unfolding on America's southern border has been captured in photographs showing the lifeless bodies of a Salvadoran father and his daughter who drowned as they attempted to cross the Rio Grande into Texas. The images show Óscar and his daughter lying face down in shallow water. The 23-month-old toddler's arm is draped around her father's neck, suggesting that she was clinging to him in her final moments.[7]

This photo instantly became a symbol of the brutality of the US border control, a case of what Hegel would have called concrete universality: the image of a singular case which evokes a global tragedy and as such calls for sympathy and action.

At the end of November 2025, Sarah Hurwitz, former chief speechwriter for Barack and Michelle Obama, said at a conference that Jewish schools should ban smartphones to keep youths from seeing the carnage in Gaza: 'I'm sorry if this is a graphic thing to say, but ... when I'm trying to make arguments in favour for Israel ... I'm talking through a wall of dead children.'[8] Even if we ignore the fact that after the 7 October Hamas attack Israel was doing exactly the same, repeatedly spreading endless combinations of the clips shot by the cameras mounted on the heads of Hamas combatants, Hurwitz's logic is terrifying: what kind of arguments are there for Israel when they are threatened by images of the carnage in Gaza? Do these clips not prove that Israeli propaganda is simply lying? In short, Hurwitz's logic is that of Groucho when, in one of the Marx brothers films, he is caught lying: 'Whom do you believe, my words or your eyes?'

The lesson is that the Left should accept the struggle for hegemony and learn to win. During Joe Biden's inauguration in 2020, there was a lone figure who stole the show by just sitting there, sticking out as an element of discord disturbing the spectacle: Bernie Sanders. The effect was not that of a person left out at a party but rather of a person who has no interest in joining. Every philosopher knows how impressed Hegel was when he saw Napoleon riding through Jena – it was like seeing the world spirit (the predominant historical tendency) riding a horse ... The fact that Bernie stole the show and that the image of him just sitting there instantly became iconic means that the true world spirit of our time was there, in the lone figure embodying scepticism about the fake normalization staged in the ceremony – there is still hope for our cause, people are aware that a more radical change is needed. Lines of separation thus seemed clearly drawn: liberal establishment embodied in Biden versus democratic socialists whose most popular representative is Bernie Sanders.

But my point here is not a political one; it concerns the inherent necessity for a general spiritual tendency to 'collapse' in a particular person. This is why one cannot reduce this 'collapse' to a form of fetishism in which a complex web of mediations appears as an immediate presence: only through such a 'collapse' does this complex web (in our case, all the tendencies and hopes that Bernie personifies) acquire a form of actuality, a positive force that sustains political engagement. If we take away this collapse we don't get the

general spirit of a world in its clean form, without any contingent empirical elements – what we get is a mess with no mobilizing force. And it is important to note the difference between this image of Bernie and the photo of a defiant Trump with blood on his ear and cheek, being rushed off stage by Secret Service agents, fist raised with an American flag in the background. Although this photo also became instantly iconic, it did not acquire the same mobilizing force as the much more modest and less spectacular photo of Bernie sitting alone.[9]

Back to our starting point: the true morbidity resided in the attempt to stage Biden's inauguration as a return to normality after the unfortunate detour of Trump's reign. The widespread appeal of the image of Bernie sitting alone was a sign that millions of people were aware of the morbidity of Biden's inauguration, and that they hope an authentic new beginning is possible.

Mamdani's Wager

Emancipatory forces all around the world rightfully enjoyed the victory of Zohran Mamdani, the first Democratic Socialist mayor of New York. Perhaps a kind of proof that it's not just the populist Right that can mobilize the crowd. However, as Mamdani himself knows very well, this victory exposes him to multiple acts of economic and financial sabotage: it is vital to the interests of the 'deep state' powers – Republican and Democratic – that his mandate should end in catastrophe. Let us not forget that Trump himself appealed to New Yorkers to vote for the Democrat Andrew Cuomo. With Mamdani in power, Trumpian populists and mainstream Democrats full of anti-Trump rhetoric are suddenly speaking the same language. The establishment will do everything they can to undermine his political downfall, including claiming a state of emergency allowing the National Guard to intervene. Thus, for the Left it's not only the time to act but also to think.

The US is now transforming itself from a two-party state into a four-party state: establishment Republicans, establishment Democrats, alt-Right populists and Democratic Socialists. There are already signs of coalitions across party lines: Joe Biden hinted that he would nominate a moderate Republican as his vice-president while Steve Bannon claimed his ideal was a coalition between Trump and Bernie Sanders. The big difference is that while Trump's populism easily asserted its hegemony over the Republican establishment (a clear indication, that, in spite of all Bannon's ranting against the 'system', that Trump is not a friend of the 'ordinary' worker), the split in the Democratic party continues apace – no wonder the struggle between the Democratic establishment and the Sanders wing is *the only true political struggle going on in the US*. As Emma Brockes wrote: 'Zohran Mamdani's biggest threat is not Donald Trump, it's the Democratic old guard.'[1] No wonder that when, towards the end of November 2025, Mamdani visited Trump in the White House, they got along very well and Trump unexpectedly praised Mamdani: what they both share is a hatred towards the soft Fascism of the establishment and a reliance on popular mobilization, although from different sides (Trump is a populist authoritarian and Mamdani an authentic Leftist).

To indulge ourselves with a bit of theoretical jargon: we are dealing with two antagonisms ('contradictions'), one between Trump and the liberal establishment (this is what Trump's impeachment during his first term was really about), and that between the Sanders wing of the Democratic Party and *all others* (including Republicans). The move to impeach Trump was a desperate attempt by the liberal establishment to regain a perceived moral leadership and credibility – a comic exercise in hypocrisy since all it did was reveal the profound inadequacies of the Democratic Party.

Trump is a monster both for the Republican establishment and for the mainstream Democrats. For the Republicans, he is a monster which made them aware that they are in themselves dead, that only Trumpian populism keeps them alive. For the mainstream Democrats, Trump is the monster which keeps them alive, or, rather, which gives them a semblance of life: their fixation on Trump as their arch-enemy is the only thing that gives them a political momentum.[2] To apply yet again the classic scene from cartoons: a cat reaches a precipice, but it goes on walking, ignoring the fact that there is no ground under its feet; it starts to fall only when it looks down and notices the abyss. In our case, the Democrats haven't yet looked down and realized that they are dead – the figure of Trump prevents them from seeing it ... This is why the public moral fervour of the Democratic establishment is ironic in the extreme. The obscenities of Trumpian politics didn't give them the principled high ground but revealed the emptiness of their own rhetoric. The Sanders' camp, on the other hand, sees this clearly: there is no way back, US political life has to be radically reinvented.

As many commentators have mentioned, Mamdani won because *he did for the Left what Trump did for the Right*: he didn't pander to the centre but adopted a position of unapologetic radicalism. The four political 'parties' I mentioned above do not operate at the same level: we have the two dying parties caught inextricably in their own inertia, lacking any serious vision (old mainstream Republicans, Democrats), then two emerging political movements – Trumpian populists, Democratic Socialists – with actual momentum and force. The only truly alive and meaningful election would be Trump versus the Democratic Socialists. Why, then, should the Democratic Socialists not split from the mainstream party? My answer to this would be to adopt a principled pragmatism: we should focus upon central goals which concern our survival, and *everything is permitted* to move towards these goals – democracy when democracy works, authoritarian state control when it is necessary, popular mobilization when it is needed, even a level of terror when things get really desperate.

This can be illustrated by looking at two recent attempts to launch new political parties. First, in July 2025, Elon Musk claimed he would launch his own party, in the aftermath of his dramatic rift with Trump the previous month: 'The billionaire announced "The American Party" on X, billing it as an overt challenge to the Republican and Democratic two-party system.' However, it appears that the supposed party still hasn't been registered with American election authorities and it isn't clear if it has any reality beyond Musk's X account. Musk, who was born outside of the US, is ineligible to run for the presidency and hasn't made clear who would lead the party or campaign for election to the White House.[3] This was Musk's attempt to outperform Trump but with technofeudalism rather than populism. Meanwhile in the UK, Zarah Sultana and Jeremy Corbyn announced the making of a new Left Party, and their project initially looked promising – according to some polls, around half of Labour voters might transfer their vote. However as properly befits a Leftist party, the two would-be leaders immediately started publicly feuding. In a European parallel to my comments on what a meaningful US election might look like, a true UK political battle would be between Farage's Reform Party and the new Leftist party, marginalizing the inert Labour and the eccentric moribund Conservatives. However, one could probably safely predict that, in such a confrontation, Farage would win in the same way Boris Johnson beat Corbyn a decade ago (although the victory of Corbyn remains his reappropriation of the Labour Party, terrifying the political establishment in the process).

So, there is no principled answer to this dilemma: there are occasions where taking control of an established political party appears wise and times when a split seems both necessary and inevitable. It could be that Mamdani did right to remain within the Democratic party, mobilizing its popular base against the Democratic establishment – if he were to take on all three other political forces in the US (old Republicans, Trumpians and the Democratic establishment), victory would have surely been impossible. It is now within his purview to take over the New York branch of the Democratic Party, establish a network not only with Democratic Socialists all around the US, but also, following Bernie Sanders' advice, to appeal to the disenfranchised poor workers and farmers who Trump so successfully commandeered. The future for Mamdani has to be sweeping up the disappointed Trumpians, not the boring inert centre. Only a radical Leftist has a chance to win over the working-class Trumpians who are totally justified in their deep-seated distrust of the political establishment.

Conclusion
Abandon All Hope, You Who Enter Radical Politics

What is the sound of wilful ignorance? In January 1948, Herbert Marcuse wrote a letter to Martin Heidegger, asking him why he had never spoken out about the Nazi terror and the murder of six million Jews, even now, after the end of the war. Heidegger responded:

> I can only add that instead of the word 'Jews' [in your letter] there should be the word 'East Germans,' and then exactly the same [terror] holds true of one of the Allies [the Soviet Union], with the difference that everything that has happened since 1945 is public knowledge world-wide, whereas the bloody terror of the Nazis was in fact kept a secret from the German people.[1]

Three years after the end of World War II and the fall of the Nazi regime, Heidegger remained insistent that the majority of German people were ignorant of the horrors perpetrated in their name. Blatantly not true: Germans *wanted* to know nothing – which means they (generally, at least) knew it but pretended not to know it.

It is this determination not to acknowledge even to themselves that they knew what they knew which is portrayed in *The Zone of Interest*, Jonathan Glazer's 2023 film, loosely based on the novel by Martin Amis. Set in 1943, it tells the story of Rudolf Höss, commandant of the Auschwitz concentration camp, who in 1943 lives with his wife Hedwig and their five children in an idyllic home next to the camp. Höss takes the children out to swim and fish, and Hedwig spends time tending the garden. Servants handle chores and the prisoners' belongings are given to the family. Beyond the garden wall, gunshots, shouting and sounds of trains and furnaces sound . . .[2] The German critic Hanns-Georg Rodek summarized the predominant reception of the film: 'Glazer describes the situation by means of details which are more oppressive than anything we've seen in Holocaust films before. It concentrates in one garden the attitude of an entire nation that wanted to know nothing.'[3]

But now comes the saddest part of the story: does this mean that the horrible suffering happening on the other side of the wall turned the victims into embittered ethical heroes? The lesson to be drawn here is a very painful one: we have to abandon the idea that there is something emancipatory in extreme experiences, that they enable us to clear the mess and open our eyes to the ultimate truth of a situation – that there is any such thing as 'perfect victims', or the truly innocent. In 1942, on the Adriatic island of Rab, the Italian military built a concentration camp where thousands of (mostly) Slovene prisoners, women and children included, were held under terrible conditions. After the war and the liberation of the camp, researchers discovered that there were tragic cases among the prisoners of mothers stealing the food from their own children in order to survive.[4]

And this sad lesson should be generalized: if one should avoid putting victims of atrocities on a pedestal as unsullied martyrs, one should also avoid idealizing them as fighters for justice. Remi Adekoya has pointed out that extensive research uncovered a strange fact: when voters were asked which value they appreciated most, in the developed West the large majority chose equality, while in sub-Saharan Africa, the large majority put wealth in first place (independently of how it was acquired, even if it was through corruption). This result makes a kind of sense: the developed West can afford to prioritize equality at the level of ideological self-perception, while the main worry among the poor majority in sub-Saharan Africa is how to survive and leave devastating poverty behind.[5]

The conclusion to be drawn from these and other similar phenomena is that one of the basic premises of the contemporary Left – the inherent link between freedom and equality – should be abandoned. In order to emphasize this link, Etienne Balibar condensed the two terms into one: *egaliberte* ('freequality', one might put it in English, although this doesn't quite work – it could be read as 'free quality'). Badiou opposes Balibar's maneouvre, choosing equality at the expense of freedom, but both Balibar and Badiou are going against Marx who, many will be surprised to learn, dismisses equality. The famous lines 'From each according to his ability, to each according to his needs!', as Marx writes in *The Critique of the Gotha Program* (1875), have a fundamental presupposition, which is that human beings have unequal abilities and unequal needs:

> one worker is married, another is not; one has more children than another, and so on and so forth. Thus, with an equal performance of labor, and hence an equal in the social consumption fund, one will in fact receive more than another, one will be richer than another, and so on. To avoid all these defects, right, instead of being equal, would have to be unequal.[6]

What kind of equality do we crave? Equality in one category inevitably brings about inequality in another. People belonging to different cultures will always be different. People with different skills cannot be made equal. Marx does not deny this: the aim of the revolution is, for him, not to impose equality but to achieve the abolition of class *exploitation*. To put it brutally, for Marx, inequality remains even after the revolution.

In his memoir on his debilitating illness, Hanif Kureishi wrote the fateful sentence: 'Work liberates us.' (A literal translation of '*Arbeit macht frei*' at the entrance to Auschwitz – true, with the addition of 'us'.) Kureishi then goes on to dwell on the liberating effect of writing: 'We are making a contribution to the world; our art is for others and not for ourselves alone; a connection is being made. This is the spark of life, a kind of love. We should be able to enjoy our successes and love ourselves in proportion to them.'[7] Could this explanation also be appropriated by Nazis, claiming that keeping the prisoners in conditions of horror is also making a contribution to the world? In principle, why not? The space of ideological manipulation is limitless.

Back to *The Zone of Interest*: Glazer did not want the atrocities occurring inside the camp to be seen, only heard. He described the film's sound as 'the other film' and 'arguably, *the* film'. But what about the opposite – not sounds without proper images accompanying them but images without the sound that belongs to them? Jorge Semprun reports how he witnessed the arrival of a truckload of Polish Jews at Buchenwald; they were packed into the freight train, almost two hundred to a car, travelling for days without food and water in the coldest winter of the war. On arrival, everybody in one carriage had frozen to death except for fifteen children, kept warm by the others in the centre of the bundle of bodies. When the children were taken from the car, the Nazis let their dogs loose on them. Soon only two fleeing children were left:

> The little one began to fall behind, the SS were howling behind them and then the dogs began to howl too, the smell of blood was driving them mad, and then the bigger of the two children slowed his pace to take the hand of the smaller ... together they covered a few more yards ... till the blows of the clubs felled them and, together they dropped, their faces to the ground, their hands clasped for all eternity.[8]

What should not escape our attention is that the freeze of eternity is embodied in the hand as partial object: while the bodies of the two boys perish, the clasped hands persist for all eternity like the smile of the Cheshire cat from *Alice in Wonderland*. One can easily imagine this scene cinematically: while the soundtrack renders reality in the sounds of the two children being clubbed to death, the camera lingers on a still shot of their clasped hands, immobilized for eternity – while the sound renders temporary reality, the image renders the eternal real. It is the pure surface of such fixed images of eternity, not any deeper meaning, which allows for redemptive moments in the bleak story of the Shoah. If Glazer's film renders the horror only through sound and thereby renders it, in its very invisibility, as an oppressive omnipresence with no redemptive hope in view, the imagined cinema version of Semprun's fragment maybe gives rise to some hope.

So can we also imagine such a small redemptive scene in *The Zone of Interest*? One of the minor characters is a Polish girl who lives near the camp: she sneaks out every night, hiding food at the prisoners' work sites for them to find and eat. (The scenes with her distributing food are shot in black-and-white – a stylistic reversal of the doomed girl in a red coat running around when the Nazis are clearing the Krakow ghetto in Spielberg's *Schindler's List*, and in both cases it doesn't work because it comes all too close to a rather vulgar metaphor.) What if, however, towards the end of the film, we were to see her putting an apple on a pile of earth, followed by the voice of a soldier approaching and the snarling of an attacking dog while the girl utters a terrified scream – but what we see is a still image of her hand holding the apple, frozen as an eternal monument to human compassion? In dark times like ours, we need such small miracles.

The darkness of our era is easy to see. Walter Benjamin is credited with the statement: 'Behind every fascism is a failed revolution.' This statement (to which I myself referred at least ten times, including once already in this book) obviously offers itself as the formula that could account for ongoing Conservative populism (not only of the Trumpian variety): hegemonic liberal democracy failed to perceive the discontent of the silent majority of the working class which didn't recognize itself in the topics of multiculturalism, woke-ism and identity politics; neo-fascist populists filled in this gap and presented themselves as the voice of the working class exploited by the liberal elite ... However, this formula doesn't address the key enigma: *why* did revolution fail, i.e., why did the new Right and not the Left succeed in capturing the rage and fury of many so-called ordinary people? Lately it has become quite popular to blame theory (philosophy) which failed to offer the exploited majority a viable political programme able to mobilize the people. Otto Paans (in his otherwise very perspicuous analysis) argues:

> One cannot expect academics working within an ideological frame with largely pre-selected topics of inquiry, focused on multiculturalism, enlightened-lite atheism, and simplistic egalitarianism to provide sound political alternatives to contemporary demands. No wonder that Enlightenment Lite left liberals, and especially professional academic philosophers, *have been completely bowled over* by Trump's election: regression to a neo-fascist dictatorship was not something that they ever even remotely anticipated. [...] *[P]rofessional academic philosophy has a moral duty to change direction radically*, because

the absence of real, serious philosophy diminishes virtually to zero the chances of genuine political change or resistance against intellectual dictatorship in either of its *politically correct* or *neo-fascist* sub-species.[9]

Simple and convincing – but is Paans' request not a permanent motif of (what remains of) today's radical Left? Paans refers to Adorno and Horkheimer as great authorities, but did *they* provide a more consistent answer? In one of his late short texts, Adorno gives a clear answer to the question 'So what should we do today?': 'I don't know.' And is it not the same with Paans' text itself? He insists that 'professional academic philosophy' should provide a concrete programme *without giving any clear indication of what this programme should be*. What we get are ultimately just two options: the 'realist' pragmatism of the Third Way liberal Left and, from circles linked to the Third World, a rehabilitation of 'really-existing Socialism' (up to a new, more positive appraisal of not just Mao but also Stalin) – in this view, the original sin of western Marxism was that it lost contact with revolutionary movements outside the developed capitalist countries. My position here is exactly the opposite one: western Marxism was right in rejecting any continuity with 'really-existing Socialism' which was, all in all, a gigantic failure – it succeeded economically only by integrating moments of capitalism. Our only realistic option is therefore to fully accept this absence of an actual alternative, of the deadlock poignantly expressed in a message I recently got from a young friend in Japan (online name Cabin):

> I would like to know whether you have noticed the Japanese House of Councillors election that has just taken place. The far-right political party, the '参政党', has achieved an unprecedented victory by winning 14 seats. In the statistical results, the majority of the voters are young people. The far-right has gained huge momentum among the young by posting a large number of rumors about foreigners or other things on social media through a massive number of paid posters. Meanwhile, on the streets of Kyoto, the sincere but already aged left-wing elderly men and women in their seventies and eighties are making speeches and propagating their ideas on the hot temperature, but to little avail.

CONCLUSION

What do you think of this reversal? Has the world become old? As young people, how should we face this situation? Has there been such a period in history? To be honest, I almost no longer believe that the world can be changed. I almost feel that people in today's capitalist society are coddled, and as a result, they are fragile, short-sighted, and extreme, eventually becoming a breeding ground for the far right. I feel that those left-wing elderly people on the streets of Kyoto, who truly believe that they can change the world, are 'much younger' than me. As young people, what should we do in the face of such a situation? In the next few years, I will study and live in Japan. Faced with such a rightward trend, I feel a sense of powerlessness – where can I escape to? There is no new continent left for us.

Yes, we should fully accept the conclusion: there is no place we can escape to, no new continent left for us. When, in *Munich: The Edge of War* (2021), someone tries to convince a German diplomat who plans to kill Hitler that violent resistance doesn't work, and that we should stick to endless negotiations which keep hope alive, the German diplomat replies: 'Hoping is waiting for someone else to do it. We'd all be much better off without it.' This is what I meant with the title of my book (taken from a text by Giorgio Agamben), *The Courage of Hopelessness*: true radical politics is like Dante's Hell, above the entrance to which a placard reads, '*Lasciate ogne speranza, voi ch'intrate*' (usually translated as 'Abandon all hope, ye who enter here'). It is ridiculous to blame academic philosophy for this hopelessness: the situation itself, the way we experience it, offers no perspective. While a radical change is needed, it is simultaneously impossible (again, in our reality).

Following the Stalinist turn, Communist revolutions were grounded in a clear vision of historical reality ('scientific socialism'), its laws and tendencies, so that, in spite of all its unpredictable twists, the revolution was fully located into this process of historical reality – as they liked to say, Socialism should be built in each country according to its particular conditions, but in accordance with general laws of history. In theory, revolution was thus deprived of the dimension of subjectivity proper, of radical cuts of the real into the texture of 'objective reality' – in clear contrast to the French

Revolution whose most radical figures perceived it as an open process lacking any support in a higher necessity. Saint-Just wrote in 1794: *'Ceux qui font des révolutions ressemblent au premier navigateur instruit par son audace'* ('Those who make revolutions resemble a first navigator, who has audacity alone as a guide').[10] Today, even more than in Lenin's time, we navigate uncharted territories, without a global cognitive mapping – but what if this lack of cognitive mapping is what enbles us to avoid totalitarian closure?[11]

What our situation demands is clear. A non-negotiable component of any Left is universalism – if for no other reason, then for the simple fact that today's 'late capitalist' society (the often-used predicate 'late' is in itself meaningless, it rather signals our ignorance) is globally interconnected to an extent unthinkable until now. To avoid yet another listing of the obvious cases (global threat to our environment, the impact of AI, the prospect of social chaos and military self-destruction), suffice it to mention how even things which were once a state monopoly are now part of international trade. Trump has repeatedly floated sending American prisoners to serve prison sentences outside the country – this time threatening to send the people charged with vandalizing Teslas to Ecuador.[12] So you can serve your prison term in a country where the act for which you were condemned is not a criminal offence! Ghana and Serbia are preparing to sign a landmark Memorandum of Understanding on labour mobility, which will enable 100,000 Ghanaian workers to benefit from Serbia's work permit programme this year. (The deal was later cancelled.)[13] The same thing happened back in 1970 when the GDR imported thousands of workers from Vietnam (which took part of the salary earned by these workers). Again, workers are sold by state to another state ... North Korea brought this logic to its extremes, basically selling thousands of soldiers to Russia where they fight on the front and are dying in droves. (Would it not be much more appropriate for North Korea to sell its workers to South Korea which doesn't have enough of them? For ideological reasons, this is of course impossible ...)

How, then, are we to act in such a messy global situation? I'll take a risk and present here what I cannot resist calling my realist utopia.[14] The daily run of things is best done by some

CONCLUSION

moderately-conservative force – they are pragmatic enough to avoid excessive risks, always ready to take into account how even the best projects can go wrong. In short, they know that in politics the agent has to take full responsibility: a true politician should never say 'I meant it well, just the unfortunate circumstances ruined it all.' However, such an approach is not enough to cope with the prospect of inevitable catastrophes that haunt entire humanity – this is why a kind of new Leninist elite is needed, a group whose main task is not to elaborate old-fashioned Communist dreams but to make all of us ready for the impending catastrophes, i.e., to keep us aware that we are approaching a global emergency state. My utopia is thus a silent coalition between moderate conservatives (who run day-to-day things) and a Leninist elite (which prepares us for the impending breakdown) – but I am well aware that today both these agents are disappearing from the political scene. Moderate conservatives are being swept aside by Trumpian populists, whatever remains of the radical Left is caught in a fake peacenik utopianism.

Insofar as even this crazy dream is all too utopian, what should we do? My formula is one of principled pragmatism: we should focus on central goals which concern our survival, and *everything is permitted* to move towards these goals – democracy when democracy works, authoritarian state control when it is necessary, popular mobilization when it is needed, even a level of terror when things get really desperate. In his *Notes Towards a Definition of Culture*, the great conservative T. S. Eliot made an often-quoted remark: there are moments when the only choice is the one between heresy and non-belief, when the only way to keep a religion alive is to perform a sectarian split from its main corpse. Lenin did this with regard to traditional Marxism, Mao did this in his own way, and Deng with Mao ... all of them with mixed results. Today, the Left has so far failed to do it – it was Trump that enacted a heretic break with global neoliberalism. Again, there should be no prejudices here: we should be ready to take from the enemy topics like patriotism, defence of our specific way of life, family life included ... So we do need a heresy, but a heresy that will work, with a chance of becoming hegemonic, not a new, small faction proud of telling the truth although this truth is largely ignored, not a party trembling at each election. Mamdani's victory in New York makes it clear that a heresy can work. So, to paraphrase what Che Guevara said about Vietnam, we now need dozens of Mamdanis, not only in the US but all around the world. And then ... *voyons voir*, as they say in French: let's wait and see what there is to see. Such waiting is not just a passive observation, it demands the effort to locate focal points of our present. So where is today the focal point at which all our antagonisms and threats to survival converge, a singular point which stands for our universal deadlock? Not Gaza, not Ukraine, not Sudan, not even north Myanmar, but *Tehran*.

Tehran is inexorably facing a 'Day Zero' when it will simply run out of water. And it's not just Tehran – most of Iran is driven towards 'water bankruptcy', the point where water demand permanently exceeds the supply and nature can't keep up. The situation is so dire that Iranian President Masoud Pezeshkian revived a long-debated plan to move the capital from the Tehran metropolitan area, which is home to fifteen million people. In November 2025, he took a step further and framed relocation as a mandate, not as a choice: the city will become uninhabitable.

The reasons are multiple. The immediate cause is a severe drought afflicted Iran in the past four years: even in the rainy season there was practically no rain. Then there is the fact that Iran has relied heavily on water-intensive irrigation to grow food in dry landscapes and subsidized water and energy use, resulting in overpumping from aquifers and falling groundwater supplies. Then there is the concentration of economic activity and employment in major urban centres, particularly Tehran, which has also catalysed massive migration and thus further strained already overstretched water resources. The dwindling of the groundwater supplies caused the sinking of the entire Tehran plateau by on average 35 cm per year, which means that even if plentiful rains did come soon, it would not remain as groundwater but will be lost. Furthermore, different parts of Tehran are sinking at different speeds, so that the entire water and irrigation system is falling apart, underground tubes rupture, gas leaks into the open air.[15]

The regime has been aware of this problem for decades, but they have postponed again and again any serious attempt to deal with it – why? Because the nation's resources were spent on the nuclear

CONCLUSION

industry and its proxies, as well as on military production (selling drones that bomb Ukraine to Russia, keeping the army well equipped). Now that the water crisis has become unignorable, the Revolutionary Guard (the brutal arm of the regime) created a 'water mafia' and a 'lithium mafia', which has led to the drying up of Iran's oldest lakes and rivers that have survived for thousands of years: the mafia was stealing water from the lakes and selling it to individuals in Tehran, so that an average family is now spending 10 per cent of their income on buying water. Since water is expensive, many people cannot take a bath, elementary hygiene is plummeting.

The regime is thus directly profiting from the crisis. But we should also raise the question: why is this ongoing problem now coming up in the global news? Is it because the West wants to make the world ready for their next Israeli-American attack masked as yet another humanitarian intervention? Netanyahu cynically offered help, promising to flood Iran with specialists to help normalize the water situation just as soon as Iran was 'free' – why not now, when help is really needed?

And, now that the crisis is out in the open, what is the regime doing apart from organizing mass prayers for rain? They took a very risky decision: planes are spreading massive amounts of salt and other chemicals in the atmosphere above big cities that are supposed to create clouds and thus bring rain. However, this cloud seeding doesn't work: salt just spreads in the air and falls down to earth, killing off masses of vegetation and making breathing very difficult, so that people prefer to stay at home and society is falling apart, not just in Tehran but also in other big cities like Tabriz where universities only offer classes via Zoom.

Pezeshkian's plan to move the capital to the south-east is ambiguous: does he mean just the government administration or the bulk of the population? If he intends the first (as is the case in Myanmar), what will happen to the remaining millions? If it is the second, then this project will take long years and put an insupportable financial burden on the state without solving the present problem. Tens of thousands in Tehran are already reacting in panic: highways north from the Tehran area are jammed with cars moving towards the coastal region of the Caspian Sea where there is still enough water. What will follow if the panic goes on, where will millions move? Turkey is the obvious first candidate, and then Europe ... But what about rich Arab countries around the gulf? Why are the neighbours of Iran not expected to provide real help?

Although the water crisis in Iran is the result of a specific mixture of causes, this crisis has a global dimension. The signs are that similar threats are already arising in other countries close to Iran. Although Afghanistan is now engaged in giant irrigation projects, Kabul is also getting close to water bankruptcy – not to mention the fact that these irrigation projects are perceived by countries around Afghanistan as a threat to their survival (similar to dams on the Upper Nile in Ethiopia, which pose a threat to Egypt whose very survival depends on the Nile water supply) ... While I don't have any concrete proposals of what to do, the general solution seems clear: some form of Communism.

By Communism I don't mean any form of the twentieth-century 'actually existing socialism', but something much more obvious and elementary – something which was already tried during the Covid epidemic, but failed. Neither authoritarian state nor multi-party democracy or grassroots self-organization will work. When we are facing threats to our very survival as a civilized community, there is no other way than to proclaim a large-scale emergency state, and emergency state means a de facto war, not against another state but against those who are responsible for the water crisis in our own country. The emergency state should not 'abolish the market' and nationalize everything, but it should put under public control and regulate many key moments of social life beginning (in this situation) with controlled distribution of water. (What the 'water mafia' is doing now in Iran should have been crushed in a direct and brutal way.) Strong state power able to act quickly should be combined with locally-organized acts of solidarity. Much stronger international cooperation is also needed.

A utopia? Maybe, but the true utopia is the idea that we can survive without such measures. The outlined vision of a new Communism is utopian in the precise sense that it is not grounded in a detailed analysis of the past but in what one should take the risk of calling *signs from the future*. What goes on now in Tehran is

CONCLUSION

such a sign from the future: a detail which indicates where we are going to end if we do not act decisively now. The main task of materialist prophesying is to learn to read such signs from the future: in the destruction of our environment, in wars exploding all around, in the glitches of AI ... Without reading signs from the future that are signalling us that we are lost if we go on like we are doing now, we are really lost.

Notes

Introduction

1. See Jonah Goldberg, *Liberal Fascism: The Secret History of the Left from Mussolini to the Politics of Meaning* (London: Penguin, 2009).
2. See *Zero Point* (London: Bloomsbury, 2025) for a full explanation of the meaning of this term.
3. I tried to elaborate this antagonism in my *Freedom: A Disease Without Cure* (London: Bloomsbury, 2023).
4. Svetlana Reiter and Investigations Team, 'British and US bestsellers hit by purge in Russian bookshops', BBC News, 29 May 2025 (https://www.bbc.com/news/articles/cdj98zg2xkeo).
5. J. Oliver Conroy, 'Book burning, Latin prayers – and a lot of kids: inside the American "trad family" movement', *The Guardian*, 30 August 2025 (https://www.theguardian.com/lifeandstyle/ng-interactive/2025/aug/30/trad-families-modern-life).
6. Stalin, *Dialectical and Historical Materialism*, September 1938, accessed via marxists.org (https://www.marxists.org/reference/archive/stalin/works/1938/09.htm).
7. Op. cit.
8. See Slavoj Žižek, *Against Progress* (London: Bloomsbury, 2024).
9. I rely here on the ideas of Alex Taek-Gwang Lee, Seoul.
10. Confucius, *Analects*, Book XIII, 3:4–7, accessed via Wikipedia, 'Rectification of names' (https://en.wikipedia.org/wiki/Rectification_of_names).
11. See my writing on this in *Disparities* (London: Bloomsbury, 2016).
12. Plato, *The Republic*, Book 1, trans. Benjamin Jowett, accessed via The Internet Classics Archive (https://classics.mit.edu/Plato/republic.2.i.html).

13. Not to embarrass well-meaning critics, I prefer not to give concrete names.
14. Melina Walling and Seth Borenstein, 'Trump called climate change a "con job" at the United Nations. Here are the facts and context', PBS News, 25 September 2025 (https://www.pbs.org/newshour/politics/trump-called-climate-change-a-con-job-at-the-united-nations-here-are-the-facts-and-context).
15. Plato, *The Republic*, Book 1.
16. Nick Paton Walsh, 'China tells EU it can't accept Russia losing its war against Ukraine, official says', CNN, 4 July 2025 (https://edition.cnn.com/2025/07/04/europe/china-ukraine-eu-war-intl).

Altona, Los Angeles: From the Nearby to the Neighbour

1. ET Online, 'Israel–Iran conflict: "Iran can never have a nuclear weapon", G7 says', *The Economic Times*, 17 June 2025 (https://economictimes.indiatimes.com/news/defence/israel-iran-conflict-g7-leaders-including-trump-urge-de-escalation-on-iran/articleshow/121898800.cms?from=mdr).
2. Agencies, 'Germany's Merz says Israel is doing the "dirty work for all of us" by countering Iran', *The Times of Israel*, 17 June 2025 (https://www.timesofisrael.com/liveblog_entry/germanys-merz-says-israel-is-doing-the-dirty-work-for-all-of-us-by-countering-iran/).
3. See https://germanhistorydocs.org/en/nazi-germany-1933-1945/correspondence-between-wilhelm-furtwaengler-and-joseph-goebbels-about-art-and-the-state-april-1933
4. It is worth mentioning here that, before becoming a politician, Hitler was a painter, so that his move from painting to politics is just a move from one to another form of art.
5. Andrew Roth, 'Republican hawks vs MAGA isolationists: the internal war that could decide Trump's Iran response', *The Guardian*, 17 June 2025 (https://www.theguardian.com/us-news/2025/jun/17/republican-hawks-vs-maga-isolationists-the-internal-war-that-could-decide-trumps-iran-response).
6. Alenka Zupančič, *Paranoiac Power* (read in manuscript).
7. Peter Walker, 'Trump says UK is protected from tariffs "because I like them" as trade deal is signed off', *The Guardian*, 16 June 2025

(https://www.theguardian.com/politics/2025/jun/16/starmer-and-trump-finalise-uk-us-trade-deal-at-g7-but-steel-tariffs-still-on-hold).

8. Here is a ridiculous case of such a freedom of speech, a recent reply to my Substack text on evil being seen as evil: 'What has Slavs ever really done other than bang Melania Trump in college.'

9. Aamer Madhani and Chris Megerian, 'Trump says the US knows where Iran's Khameini is hiding and urges Iran's unconditional surrender', *AP*, 17 June 2025 (https://www.ap.org/news-highlights/spotlights/2025/trump-says-the-us-knows-where-irans-khamenei-is-hiding-and-urges-irans-unconditional-surrender/).

10. Laura Powell, 'Taxpayers subsidize LA unrest through California's "protest-industrial complex"', *The Spectator: World*, 10 June 2025 (https://thespectator.com/topic/california-taxpayers-subsidize-protest-industrial-complex-fueling-la-riots/).

11. See https://www.degruyterbrill.com/document/doi/10.4159/9780674038592-004/html?lang=en&srsltid=AfmBOoo3KwWCavLNwTd1L-tkCmluRc845vMnuPBJbgffawJJvuEDTAKN

12. Quoted in Emily Tamkin, 'Steve Bannon has given an old antisemitic trope a fresh "pro-Israel" spin', *Forward*, 25 February 2025 (https://forward.com/opinion/699337/steve-bannon-israel-antisemitic/).

13. Ibid.

14. Biao Xiang, 'The nearby: A scope of seeing', *Journal of Contemporary Chinese Art*, November 2021, Vol. 8, 2–3:147–65 (https://intellectdiscover.com/content/journals/10.1386/jcca_00042_1).

The Ambivalence of De-commodification

1. Elliot Leavy, 'DeepSeek has redefined what's possible for AI', *The Spectator: World*, 28 January 2025 (https://thespectator.com/topic/deepseek-has-redefined-possible-ai/?utm_source=Spectator%20World%20Signup&utm_campaign=195712d7da-EMAIL_CAMPAIGN_2025_01_27_11_08&utm_medium=email&utm_term=0_-195712d7da-154695757).

2. Dan Milmo, Amy Hawkins, Robert Booth and Julia Kollewe, '"Sputnik moment": $1tn wiped off US stocks after Chinese firm unveils AI chatbot', *The Guardian*, 28 January 2025 (https://www.theguardian.com/business/2025/jan/27/tech-shares-asia-europe-fall-china-ai-deepseek).

NOTES

3. Mark Sweney, 'US tech stocks partly recover after Trump says Deepseek AI chatbot is "wake-up call"', *The Guardian*, 28 January 2025 (https://www.theguardian.com/technology/2025/jan/28/donald-trump-china-deepseek-ai-chatbot-shares).

4. Ibid.

5. Jessica Hagen, 'Trump revokes Biden's executive order on responsible AI development', *MobiHealth News*, 21 January 2025 (https://www.mobihealthnews.com/news/trump-revokes-bidens-executive-order-responsible-ai-development?aliId=eyJpIjoiR3dxU1ZkV3JaQVZOdzhZMiIsInQiOiJ4NkJmMHBNNUZHQjFoZzJVZkhkQTlnPT0ifQ%253D%253D&iesrc=ctr).

6. Donna Lu, 'We tried out DeepSeek. It worked well, until we asked it about Tiananmen Square and Taiwan', *The Guardian*, 28 January 2025 (https://www.theguardian.com/technology/2025/jan/28/we-tried-out-deepseek-it-works-well-until-we-asked-it-about-tiananmen-square-and-taiwan).

7. See Zorana Baković, 'Kitajcem ne morejo preprečiti, da mislijo', *Delo*, 29 January 2025 (https://www.delo.si/mnenja/komentarji/kitajska-deepseek-umetna-inteligenca, in Slovene).

8. Yanis Varoufakis, 'Lessons from Syria: An imperialist's enemy is not always an anti-imperialist's friend', *DiEM25*, 10 December 2024 (https://diem25.org/lessons-from-syria-an-imperialists-enemy-is-not-always-an-anti-imperialists-friend/).

9. This new trend isn't confined to Big Tech: it has been quietly happening in the pharmaceutical sector as well. Akeso, a little-known Chinese biotech company, presented a new lung cancer drug, Ivonescimab, which 'was found in a trial conducted in China to have bested Keytruda, the blockbuster medication developed by Merck that has raked in more than $130 billion in sales for the American behemoth that has dominated cancer treatment'. See Wayne Chang, Will Ripley and Eric Cheung, 'A little-known Chinese company made a drug that beat the world's biggest-selling medicine', CNN Business, 25 February 2025 (https://edition.cnn.com/2025/02/25/business/china-biotech-global-disruption-intl-hnk/index.html).

10. 'Yanis Varoufakis on Cloud Capital vs AI: DeepSeek, Technofeudalism, Capitalism and the New Cold War', *DiEM25* YouTube channel, 28 January 2025 (https://www.youtube.com/watch?v=aotKmC3FHn4).

NOTES

Decolonization and the Public Use of Reason

1. Tal Shalev, 'A leaked video, a frantic search, and the top military lawyer: What to know about the scandal rocking Israel', CNN, 4 November 2025 (https://edition.cnn.com/2025/11/04/middleeast/major-general-tomer-yerushalmi-israel-intl).

2. CNN video, 'Palestinian olive pickers attacked over and over', CNN, 3 November 2025 (https://edition.cnn.com/2025/11/03/world/video/palestinian-olive-pickers-attacked-diamond-digvid).

3. Mick Krever, Isobel Yeung and Osama Alfaitouri, 'How traffickers deep in the Sahara are extorting ransom payments from refugees' families', CNN, 6 November 2025 (https://edition.cnn.com/2025/11/06/africa/traffickers-sahara-torture-ransom-libya-intl-cmd).

4. See Ivan Franceschini, Ving Li and Mark Bo, *Scam: Inside South-East Asia's Cybercrime Compounds* (London: Verso, 2025).

5. Maroosha Muzaffar, 'Mysterious case of Belarusian model "murdered" at Myanmar scam centre', *The Independent*, 23 October 2025 (https://www.independent.co.uk/asia/southeast-asia/myanmar-belarus-vera-kravtsova-bangkok-b2850608.html).

6. Ibid.

7. Ibid.

8. Ibid.

9. Benjamin Zachariah, *The Postcolonial Volk* (Cambridge: Polity Press, May 2026).

10. Wendy Ide, 'Deadpool & Wolverine review – Marvel's achingly meta new sequel is going to be huge', *The Guardian*, 27 July 2024 (https://www.theguardian.com/film/article/2024/jul/27/deadpool-wolverine-review-marvel-achingly-meta-gagfest-is-going-to-be-huge-ryan-reynolds-hugh-jackman-shawn-levy).

11. Wikipedia, '2024 Summer Olympics opening ceremony' (https://en.wikipedia.org/wiki/2024_Summer_Olympics_opening_ceremony).

12. Agenzia Nova, 'Orban: "The opening of the Olympic Games demonstrated that there is no morality in the West"', *Nova.news*, 27 July 2024 (https://www.agenzianova.com/en/news/Orban%2C-the-opening-of-the-Paris-Olympic-Games-demonstrated-that-there-is-no-morality-in-the-West/).

13. Rene Descartes, *Discourse on Method* (South Bend: University of Notre Dame Press, 1994), p. 33.

NOTES

14. In my reading of the ceremony, I rely on the observations of Alenka Zupančič and Jela Krečič.
15. Žiga Turk, X.com post (since deleted): '*Emancipiranost je evfemizem za izruvanost. Slovenost je bila praznik izruvanja Evrope iz njenega humusa. Eni to praznujejo, drugi to obžalujemo.*'
16. See Thomas Mann, *Reflections of a Nonpolitical Man* (*Betrachtungen eines Unpolitischen*) (New York: NYRB Classics, 2021).
17. Wikipedia, '*Reflections of a Nonpolitical Man*' (https://en.wikipedia.org/wiki/Reflections_of_a_Nonpolitical_Man).
18. 'Alexander Dugin and Pepe Escobar join', 24 June 2024, YouTube video, subsequently deleted (https://www.youtube.com/watch?v=fSb3yatLb5A).
19. Ibid.

Let It Rot . . .

1. Chris Lau and Hassan Tayir, 'They used to work for China's biggest companies. Now they're doing manual labour', CNN, 20 July 2024 (https://edition.cnn.com/2024/07/20/economy/china-economy-employment-blue-collar-work-intl-hnk).
2. Guy Delauney, 'Anger lingers in Serbia a year after train station tragedy', BBC, 1 November 2025 (https://www.bbc.co.uk/news/articles/ckgkk841r4eo).
3. Laurent Geslin, 'EU silent as protests in Serbia gain momentum', *Euractiv*, 1 February 2025 (https://www.euractiv.com/news/eu-silent-as-protests-in-serbia-gain-momentum/).
4. Ibid.
5. See for example, Siddhant Shah, 'Lithium before democracy: The hidden costs of Europe's green transition', *PRIF* blog, 23 July 2025 (https://blog.prif.org/2025/07/23/lithium-before-democracy-the-hidden-costs-of-europes-green-transition/).
6. Nomia Iqbal, Cecilia Macaulay and Brandon Drenon, 'Dozens of white South Africans arrive in US under Trump refugee plan', BBC, 13 May 2025 (https://www.bbc.co.uk/news/articles/crljn5046epo).
7. Mat Nashed, 'Kurdish leader Ocalan told the PKK to disband, it did: Here's what to know', Al-Jazeera, 13 May 2025 (https://www.aljazeera.com/news/2025/5/13/kurdish-leader-ocalan-told-the-pkk-to-disband-it-did-heres-what-to-know).

8. BBC, 'Turkey-Syria offensive: Not our border, says Donald Trump', BBC, 17 October 2019 (https://www.bbc.co.uk/news/world-middle-east-50075703).
9. BBC, 'Profile: Who are the Peshmerga?', BBC, 12 August 2014 (https://www.bbc.co.uk/news/world-middle-east-28738975).

Re-staging the Event

1. I resume here my own description from Slavoj Žižek, *Like a Thief in Broad Daylight* (London: Allen Lane, 2018).
2. Quoted from Susan Buck-Morss, *Dreamworld and Catastrophe* (Boston: MIT Press, 2022), p. 144.
3. Op. cit.
4. See Wikipedia's quite correct description of events – 'October Revolution', Wikipedia (https://en.wikipedia.org/wiki/October_Revolution).
5. Ibid.
6. Again, I resume here my own description from *Like a Thief in Broad Daylight*.
7. Curzio Malaparte, *Coup d'Etat: The Technique of Revolution* (London: E. P. Dutton & Co., 1932), accessed via Internet Archive (https://archive.org/details/coupdetattechniq0000curz).
8. Arvind Datar, 'The origins of "Justice must be seen to be done"', *Bar and Bench*, 18 April 2020 (https://www.barandbench.com/columns/the-origins-of-justice-must-be-seen-to-be-done).
9. Al Jazeera staff, '"We can't say we didn't know": Israeli academics demand end to war on Gaza', Al-Jazeera, 28 May 2025 (https://www.yahoo.com/news/t-didn-t-know-israeli-185420979.html).

Dark Humour in the Reign of Daddy Cool

1. Quoted in Chris Wright, 'The inspiring outrage of Norman Finkelstein', *Common Dreams*, 28 January 2023 (https://www.commondreams.org/opinion/the-inspiring-outrage-of-norman-finkelstein).
2. See Menchem Feuer, 'Zizek's comic dilemma: Kynicism or cynicism?', *Schlemiel Theory*, 30 April 2013 (https://schlemielintheory.com/2013/04/30/zizeks-comic-dilemma-kynicism-or-cynicism/).

NOTES

3. Dana Karni, Lucas Lilieholm and Oren Liebermann, 'Israel vows to escalate war with new plan to "conquer" Gaza', CNN, 6 May 2025 (https://edition.cnn.com/2025/05/05/middleeast/israel-gaza-expansion-hnk-intl).

4. G. K. Chesterton, 'The Sign of the Broken Sword', *The Innocence of Father Brown*, Project Gutenberg transcription, accessed via Standard Ebooks (https://standardebooks.org/ebooks/g-k-chesterton/the-innocence-of-father-brown/text/the-sign-of-the-broken-sword).

5. Lee Harpin, 'Yuval Noah Harari warns of "spiritual catastrophe" for Judaism', *Jewish News*, 9 June 2025 (https://www.jewishnews.co.uk/harari-warns-of-spiritual-catastrophe-for-judaism-at-unholy-stage-show-appearance/).

6. Arundhati Roy, 'The siege of Gaza is a crime against humanity. The world must intervene', text of remarks at the Munich Literature Festival on 16 November 2023, published by Scroll.in on 17 November 2023 (https://scroll.in/article/1059225/arundhati-roy-the-siege-of-gaza-is-a-crime-against-humanity-the-world-must-intervene).

7. Holly Ellyatt, 'How "Daddy" talk and Trump and Rutte's bromance stole the NATO spotlight', CNBC, 26 June 2025 (https://www.cnbc.com/2025/06/26/trump-and-ruttes-bromance-stole-the-spotlight-at-the-nato-summit.html).

8. See 'Boney M – Daddy Cool (Die aktuelle Schaubude 30.10.1976)', Boney M. YouTube channel, 16 November 2022 (https://www.youtube.com/watch?v=rYoALQp7BfY).

9. *Guardian* staff and agencies, 'Ukraine war briefing: Trump says he "didn't make any progress" with Putin after call', *The Guardian*, 4 July 2025 (https://www.theguardian.com/world/2025/jul/04/ukraine-war-briefing-trump-says-he-didnt-make-any-progress-with-putin-after-call).

10. Dan Sabbagh, 'US halts weapon shipments to Ukraine over fears its stockpiles are too low', *The Guardian*, 2 July 2025 (https://www.theguardian.com/world/2025/jul/02/us-halts-ukraine-weapons-shipments).

11. MSNBC, 'Russia fears rise of Ukraine's "gay super soldiers"', video removed by uploader (https://www.msn.com/en-gb/video/watch/russia-fears-rise-of-ukraine-s-gay-super-soldiers/vi-AA1fFnZ?ocid=msedgntp&cvid=e57d1ee687204bab9f74929d702d38a2&ei=11).

12. See Brendan Cole, 'Putin's rehabilitation of Stalin blamed for priest's blessing of statue', *Newsweek*, 19 August 2023 (https://www.newsweek.

com/putin-rehabilitation-stalin-priest-blessing-statue-russia-orthodox-1821054).
13. Israel Channel 13 News uploaded by David Sheen, 'The Miseducation of Israel', YouTube, 29 April 2019 (https://www.youtube.com/watch?v=3XB72y1Lm90).
14. As for this notion, see my *Surplus-Enjoyment* (London: Bloomsbury, 2022).
15. Julia Davis, 'Moscow terror attack: A lie too good to waste', *CEPA*, 24 March 2024 (https://cepa.org/article/moscow-terror-attack-a-lie-too-good-to-waste/).
16. Yuliya Talmazan, Larissa Gao and Caroline Radnofsky, 'Moscow attack suspects appear severely beaten as they're charged in Russian court', NBC News, 25 March 2024 (https://www.nbcnews.com/news/world/moscow-attack-suspects-beaten-charged-russian-court-torture-putin-rcna144871).
17. Pox Populi, 'The Pox Populi Guide to Creating Dissident-Nationalist Art', *Pox Populi* SubStack, 28 August 2023 (https://poxpopuli.substack.com/p/the-pox-populi-guide-to-creating?r=182myl&utm_campaign=post&utm_medium=web&triedRedirect=true).
18. Or Kashti and Gili Izikovich, '"Fire on Your Walls of Gaza": How Israel's Army Uses Revenge Poetry to Boost Morale', *Haaretz*, 26 March 2024 (https://archive.fo/l53b3).

Next Year in Gaza!

1. The Wikipedia page for the film goes through the plot in more detail (https://en.wikipedia.org/wiki/Wild_Things_(film)).
2. Quoted from Wikipedia (https://en.wikipedia.org/wiki/Wild_Things_(film)).
3. John Thorburn, 'John McNaughton's Wild Things: Pop Culture Echoes of Medea in the 1990s', in Heike Bartel (ed.), *Unbinding Medea* (New York: Routledge, 2010), p. 113.
4. See Klaus Theweleit, *Buch der Koenige, Band I: Orpheus und Euridice* (Frankfurt: Stroemfeld und Roter Stern, 1992).
5. See Wikipedia, 'Israel support for Hamas' (https://en.wikipedia.org/wiki/Israeli_support_for_Hamas).

NOTES

6. Gideon Levy, 'Recognizing Palestine won't stop the genocide in Gaza – sanctions on Israel will', *Haaretz*, 3 August 2025 (https://www.haaretz.com/opinion/2025-08-03/ty-article-opinion/.premium/recognizing-palestine-wont-stop-the-genocide-in-gaza-sanctions-on-israel-will).
7. I owe this reference to Tacitus to Hannah Wilks.
8. Wikipedia, 'Africa Corps (Russia)' (https://en.wikipedia.org/wiki/Africa_Corps_(Russia)).
9. Wikipedia, 'Afrika Korps' (https://en.wikipedia.org/wiki/Afrika_Korps).
10. Tony Kushner, *The Persistence of Prejudice: Antisemitism in British Society During the Second World War* (Manchester: Manchester University Press, 1989), p. 11.

Sumud: Remember This Word

1. Sarah Butler, 'Crime "spiralling out of control" in stores, warns British Retail Consortium', *The Guardian*, 30 January 2025 (https://www.theguardian.com/business/2025/jan/30/crime-stores-shoplifting-survey-british-retail-consortium).
2. See Alexander Smith, 'Trump says he will continue funding Ukraine's war effort – but he wants something rare in return', NBC News, 4 February 2025 (https://www.nbcnews.com/news/world/trump-says-will-continue-funding-ukraines-war-effort-wants-something-r-rcna190555).
3. Alice Cuddy and Jon Donnison, 'Trump wants neighbours to take in Palestinians to "clean out" Gaza', BBC, 26 January 2025 (https://www.bbc.co.uk/news/articles/c07kpjyzgllo).
4. Associated Press, 'Israeli Minister condemned for claiming "no such thing" as a Palestinian people', *The Guardian*, 20 March 2023 (https://www.theguardian.com/world/2023/mar/20/israeli-minister-condemned-claiming-no-such-thing-as-a-palestinian-people-bezalel-smotrich).
5. Cuddy and Donnison, 'Trump wants neighbours to take in Palestinians to "clean out" Gaza'.
6. Gur Meggido, 'Billionaire Netanyahu confidant expedited Qatari cash deliveries to Gaza, at Hamas' request', *Haaretz*, 29 March 2025

(https://www.haaretz.com/middle-east-news/2025-03-29/ty-article/.premium/netanyahu-confidant-expedited-qatari-cash-to-gaza-at-hamas-request/00000195-e395-da7e-adb7-fb9d30570000?s=03).

7. See Wikipedia, '*Sumud*' (https://en.wikipedia.org/wiki/Sumud).
8. Emma Graham-Harrison, 'Hundreds of thousands of Palestinians return to north Gaza as Israel opens checkpoints', *The Guardian*, 28 January 2025 (https://www.theguardian.com/world/2025/jan/27/israel-gaza-ceasefire-qatar-civilian-hostage-palestinians-statement).
9. The Free Press, 'Exclusive insights from former head of Mossad', The Free Press YouTube channel, 20 November 2023 (https://www.youtube.com/watch?v=OghW9UVLTk8).
10. Emma Graham-Harrison and Quique Kierszenbaum, 'Ex-Shin Bet head says Israel should negotiate with jailed intifada leader', *The Guardian*, 14 January 2024 (https://www.theguardian.com/world/2024/jan/14/shin-bet-ami-ayalon-calls-on-israel-release-intifada-leader-marwan-barghouti).
11. Personal communication with Udi Aloni.
12. See Julia Vadler, 'Trump doubles down on kicking Palestinians out of Gaza', *Politico*, 6 February 2025 (https://www.politico.eu/article/donald-trump-take-palestinians-out-of-gaza/).

Peace for Our Time

1. Elisabeth Buchwald, 'Trump announces 130% tariffs on China. The global trade war just came roaring back', CNN, 10 October 2025 (https://edition.cnn.com/2025/10/10/economy/trump-china-tariff-threats-economy).
2. Ibid.
3. Tom Edgington and Nick Eardley, 'How much have Europe and the US given to Ukraine?', BBC, 27 February 2025 (https://www.bbc.co.uk/news/articles/crew8y7pwd5o).
4. Sharon Zhang, 'Trump thanks Iran for giving advance notice of strikes on US air base in Qatar', *Truthout*, 23 June 2025 (https://truthout.org/articles/trump-thanks-iran-for-giving-advance-notice-of-strikes-on-us-air-base-in-qatar/).
5. Jake Tapper, 'Trump tells CNN Israeli forces could resume fighting in Gaza "as soon as I say the word" if Hamas won't uphold ceasefire deal',

NOTES

CNN, 16 October 2025 (https://edition.cnn.com/2025/10/15/politics/hamas-warning-trump-israel-gaza).

6. Amnesty International, 'Release Dr Hussam Abu Safiya!', Amnesty.org (https://www.amnesty.org/en/petition/release-dr-hussam-abu-safiya/).

7. Sam Sokol, 'Two MKs from mainly Arab party ejected from Knesset for holding up signs during Trump's speech; one said "Recognize Palestine" ', *The Times of Israel*, 13 October 2025 (https://www.timesofisrael.com/liveblog_entry/two-lawmakers-ejected-from-knesset-for-holding-up-signs-during-trumps-speech/).

8. Abdel Raouf Arnaout and Mohammad Sio, 'Interview – Arab lawmaker demands higher turnout to prevent Netanyahu from forming next Israeli government', AA.com, 22 October 2025 (https://www.aa.com.tr/en/middle-east/interview-arab-lawmaker-demands-higher-turnout-to-prevent-netanyahu-from-forming-next-israeli-government/3723303).

9. Myah Ward, 'Donald Trump on arresting Gavin Newsom: "I'd do it" ', *Politico*, 6 September 2025 (https://www.politico.com/news/2025/10/17/trump-still-convinced-putin-wants-to-end-this-war-lukewarm-on-zelenskyys-request-for-tomahawks-00613870).

10. Freddy Gray, 'Bannon on LA riots: "We're in World War Three" ', *The Spectator: World*, 9 June 2025 (https://thespectator.com/topic/steve-bannon-la-riots-world-war-three/?utm_source=Spectator%20World%20Signup&utm_campaign=12fd9564f8-EMAIL_CAMPAIGN_2025_06_09_08_03&utm_medium=email&utm_term=0_-12fd9564f8-154695757).

11. Bannon, op. cit.

12. Ward, 'Donald Trump on arresting Gavin Newsom'.

13. Robert Tait, 'No more "woke" in the US military: key takeaways from Pete Hegseth's speech', *The Guardian*, 30 September 2025 (https://www.theguardian.com/us-news/2025/sep/30/pete-hegseth-speech-takeaways).

14. Ellen Gamerman, 'Inside the creation of Tilly Norwood, the AI actress freaking out Hollywood', *The Wall Street Journal*, 6 December 2025 (https://www.wsj.com/arts-culture/film/tilly-norwood-ai-actress-particle6-d5c51da9?gaa_at=eafs&gaa_n=AWEtsqc2Wjt2MO8AEKqeZJdc-jyb6Snthui5vd2UA36qiMoaG-96IUvtKuTKWBqG3nA%3D&gaa_ts=693b39a1&gaa_sig=8ZNM-zNWpwxM93NOpmjcfersUtxzkMb_EWaUNvZn2_mKt3eDJlTKBp842ThDJ6lc9EkPZGZ8Sq1cCpLQQJfg4Q%3D%3D).

NOTES

15. Haley Britzky, Zachary Cohen and Natasha Bertrand, 'Hegseth pushes to remake the military in his preferred image', CNN, 1 October 2025 (https://edition.cnn.com/2025/09/30/politics/hegseth-speech-culture-standards).

16. EEAS press team, 'Russia: Statement by the spokesperson on the withdrawal from the European Convention for the Prevention of Torture and Inhuman or Degrading Treatment or Punishment', EEAS, 30 September 2025 (https://www.eeas.europa.eu/eeas/russia-statement-spokesperson-withdrawal-european-convention-prevention-torture-and-inhuman-or_en).

17. Wafaa Shurafa, Bassem Mroue and Fatma Khaled, 'Trump tells Israel to stop bombing Gaza after Hamas accepts parts of his peace plan', PBS, 3 October 2025 (https://www.independent.co.uk/news/world/americas/us-politics/trump-hegseth-military-speeches-reaction-b2836907.html).

18. Ibid.

19. See Fredric Jameson, *American Utopia* (London: Verso, 2016).

20. For a more detailed argumentation, see Fredric Jameson et al., *An American Utopia: Dual Power and the Universal Army,* ed. Slavoj Žižek (London: Verso, 2016).

The Story of Three Faces

1. CNN, 'Putin makes faces as journalists ask about Ukraine', CNN, 15 August 2025 (https://edition.cnn.com/2025/08/15/politics/video/trump-putin-alaska-summit-facial-expression-vrtc).

2. See https://www.politico.com/news/2025/12/23/this-is-shattering-europe-reels-from-trumps-new-world-order-00703927

3. See Middle East Eye, '"You don't care how many die": Piers Morgan grills Israeli settler leader Daniella Weiss', Middle East Eye YouTube channel, 17 July 2025 (https://www.youtube.com/watch?v=61MmsY9bYQQ).

4. Middle East Eye, '"Jews will go to Gaza": Israeli settler leader Daniella Weiss in new BBC documentary', Middle East Eye YouTube channel, 28 April 2025 (https://www.youtube.com/watch?v=sc5s-baywv4).

5. Arab News, 'Israelis' nomination of extremist settler leader for Nobel Peace Prize sparks online furor', Arab News, 11 March 2025 (https://www.arabnews.com/node/2593255/media).

6. CNN, 'Israeli minister taunts high-profile Palestinian prisoner', 15 August 2025 (https://edition.cnn.com/2025/08/15/world/video/ben-gvir-marwan-bargouti-taunts-prisoner-israel-vrtc-ldn-digvid).

7. Ibid.

8. Emma Graham-Harrison and Quique Kierszenbaum, 'Ex-Shin Bet head says Israel should negotiate with jailed intifada leader', *The Guardian*, 14 January 2024 (https://www.theguardian.com/world/2024/jan/14/shin-bet-ami-ayalon-calls-on-israel-release-intifada-leader-marwan-barghouti).

9. Op. cit.

Let's Pray Trump Survives

1. Alain Badiou / Elisabeth Roudinesco, 'Appel aux psychanalystes. Entretien avec Eric Aeschimann', *Le Nouvel Observateur*, 19 April 2012.

2. See Walter Lippmann, *Public Opinion* (London: George Allen & Unwin, 1922), accessed via Internet Archive (https://archive.org/details/in.ernet.dli.2015.126489).

3. See Zachary B. Wolf, 'What FDR built, Trump wants to tear down', CNN, 5 April 2025 (https://edition.cnn.com/2025/04/05/politics/what-fdr-built-trump-wants-to-tear-down/index.html).

4. Nikolay Sarkisyan, '"Cadres decide everything" – and they shape history, too', Museum of Revolution website, 25 May 2025 (https://museumsofrevolution.mml.ox.ac.uk/2025/05/25/cadres-decide-everything-and-they-shape-history-too/).

5. Lauren Aratani and David Smith, 'Trump announces sweeping new tariffs, upending decades of US trade policy', *The Guardian*, 2 April 2025 (https://www.theguardian.com/us-news/2025/apr/02/trump-new-tariffs-liberation-day).

6. Julia Frankel, 'Oscar-winning Palestinian director is attacked by Israeli settlers and detained by the army', AP News, 25 March 2025 (https://apnews.com/article/no-other-land-oscar-israel-palestinians-084c63f33e748a3279646759e9b705c2).

7. Hannah Arendt, 'The Concentration Camps', in *Partisan Review*, July 1948.

8. Michael Williams, 'Trump targets "improper ideology" at the Smithsonian in latest effort to reshape the arts and history', CNN,

28 March 2025 (https://edition.cnn.com/2025/03/28/politics/trump-targets-ideology-at-the-smithsonian/index.html).

9. All Milner quotes are from Jean-Claude Milner, 'On Some Paradoxes of Social Analysis', *Crisis & Critique*, Vol. 10, 1 (2023): 243–245.

10. Max Matza, 'Utah primary schools ban Bible for "vulgarity and violence"', BBC, 3 June 2023 (https://www.bbc.co.uk/news/world-us-canada-65794363).

11. Patrick Wintour, 'JD Vance stuns Munich conference with blistering attack on Europe's leaders', *The Guardian*, 14 February 2025 (https://www.theguardian.com/us-news/2025/feb/14/jd-vance-stuns-munich-conference-with-blistering-attack-on-europes-leaders).

12. Op. cit.

13. Saskya Vandoorne, 'French space researcher denied entry to the US over messages about Trump, French minister says', CNN, 20 March 2025 (https://edition.cnn.com/2025/03/20/europe/french-researcher-expelled-trump-intl-latam/index.html).

14. I owe this reference to Işık Barış Fidaner, Istanbul. See also http://birgun.net/politics_index.php?news_code=1328479811&year=2012&month=02&day=06

15. Extremes meet, opposite extremes have much in common. See *Oxford Reference* (https://www.oxfordreference.com/display/10.1093/oi/authority.20110803095805977).

Grab 'em by the Pussy

1. Mick Krever and Mostafa Salem, '"Trump Gaza is finally here!": US president promotes Gaza plan in AI video', CNN, 26 February 2025 (https://edition.cnn.com/2025/02/26/world/trump-promotes-gaza-plan-ai-video-intl/index.html).

2. Abeer Salman, Mohammad Al Sawalhi, Ibrahim Dahman, Niamh Kennedy and Sana Noor Haq, '"We don't want aid. We want dignity." Airdropped aid kills 3-year-old Palestinian boy in Gaza, family says', CNN, 22 October 2024 (https://edition.cnn.com/2024/10/21/middleeast/israel-gaza-airdropped-aid-kills-palestinian-child-intl/index.html).

3. I owe the translation to Jamil Khader.

4. Owen Jones, '"Kill ALL MEN In Gaza": Netanyahu Ally's Genocidal Demand Gets No Media Coverage', Owen Jones YouTube channel, 25 February 2025 (https://www.youtube.com/watch?v=gKjvJhlmBM0).

NOTES

5. Jamil Khader, *The Hasbara Glitch* (quoted from a manuscript).
6. Op. cit.
7. Jean-Claude Milner, *Relire la Revolution* (Lagrasse: Verdier, 2016), p. 246.
8. Simon Montefiore, *Stalin. The Court of the Red Tsar* (London: Weidenfeld & Nicolson, 2003), p. 168.
9. See Alexei Yurchak's wonderful *Everything Was Forever, Until It Was No More* (Princeton: Princeton University Press, 2006), p. 52.
10. See Associated Press, 'WATCH: Full exchange between Trump, JD Vance and Zelensky during Oval Office meeting', AP News YouTube channel, 28 February 2025 (https://www.youtube.com/watch?v=XVW5unmuL7I).
11. Al Jazeera, 'World reacts after Donald Trump, JD Vance berate Ukraine's Zelensky', Al Jazeera, 28 February 2025 (https://www.aljazeera.com/news/2025/2/28/world-reacts-after-donald-trump-jd-vance-berate-ukaines-zelenskyy).
12. Betsy Klein, 'US national security advisor offers his account of telling Zelensky to leave the White House', CNN, 1 March 2025 (https://edition.cnn.com/politics/live-news/trump-zelensky-ukraine-news-03-01-25#cm7q9xy9d000d3b6mjcimpod5).
13. Owen Jones, 'Media CONNING you on Starmer's Trump trip "success"', Owen Jones YouTube channel, 28 February 2025 (https://www.youtube.com/watch?v=jHwaVLBEQy8).
14. Andrew Roth and Luke Harding, 'Trump says Putin launching massive strike on Ukraine is "what anybody would do"', *The Guardian*, 7 March 2025 (https://www.theguardian.com/us-news/2025/mar/07/trump-says-it-is-easier-to-deal-with-russia-and-putin-wants-to-end-the-war).
15. Daniel Dale, 'Fact check: 33 times Zelensky thanked Americans and US leaders', CNN, 28 February 2025 (https://edition.cnn.com/2025/02/28/politics/volodymyr-zelensky-thankful-us-fact-check).
16. Anna Cooban, 'America says there are "extraordinary" economic opportunities in Russia. Really?', CNN, 1 March 2025 (https://edition.cnn.com/2025/03/01/business/economic-opportunities-us-russia-intl/index.html).
17. See Slavoj Žižek, 'Fate no longer smiles on us, Europeans', *Žižek's Goads and Prods* SubStack, 18 February 2025 (https://slavoj.substack.com/p/fate-no-longer-smiles-on-us-europeans).

18. Wikipedia, 'Donald Trump *Access Hollywood* tape' (https://en.wikipedia.org/wiki/Donald_Trump_Access_Hollywood_tape).

19. Ali Vitali, Kasie Hunt and Frank Thorp V, 'Trump referred to Haiti and African nations as "shithole" countries', NBC News, 11 January 2018 (https://www.nbcnews.com/politics/white-house/trump-referred-haiti-african-countries-shithole-nations-n836946).

20. BBC News, '"Complete, utter disaster": Lindsey Graham reacts to Zelensky meeting', BBC, 28 February 2025 (https://www.bbc.co.uk/news/videos/cx2g7yedg74o).

21. Tucker Carlson, X post, @TuckerCarlson X account, 1 March 2025 (https://x.com/TuckerCarlson/status/1895883813223354871).

22. John Ganz, 'A real war: How the Ukrainian war is being proxied', *Unpopular Front* SubStack, 11 June 2022 (https://www.unpopularfront.news/p/a-real-war?utm_campaign=post&utm_medium=web&hide_intro_popup=true).

23. Alexandra Hutzler, 'Trump and Zelensky key takeaways: Oval Office meeting explodes into shouting match', ABC News, 28 February 2025 (https://abcnews.go.com/Politics/key-takeaways-tempers-flare-trump-vance-confront-ukraines/story?id=119299758).

Why Evil Men Need Noble Spirits

1. All quotes are taken from Franz Kafka, 'The Judgement', trans. Ian Johnston (https://www.kafka-online.info/-the-judgement.html).

2. See the Wikipedia page for 'The Judgement', https://en.wikipedia.org/wiki/The_Judgment

3. David Maddox and Jane Dalton, 'Trump claims UK and Europe "going to hell" in extraordinary UN rant', *The Independent*, 23 June 2025 (https://www.independent.co.uk/news/uk/politics/trump-britain-europe-immigration-united-nations-b2832135.html).

4. Henri Bergson, *Oeuvres* (Paris: PUF, 1991), pp. 1110–1111.

5. Bergson, ibid.

6. Bergson, op. cit., p. 1340.

7. See the video clips in Anthony Blair, 'Ukrainian refugee Iryna Zarutska's look of horror after she was fatally stabbed on train – as her final moments are revealed', *New York Post*, 9 September 2025 (https://nypost.com/2025/09/09/us-news/ukrainian-refugee-

iryna-zarutskas-look-of-horror-after-she-was-fatally-stabbed-on-train-as-her-final-moments-are-revealed/).

8. See Mojca Pišek, 'Socialistični reformator Charlie Kirk', *Delo*, 26 September 2025, p. 7.

9. See Curtis Yarvin, *The Reset* (manuscript).

10. Freddy Gray, 'Bannon on LA riots: "We're in World War Three"', *The Spectator: World*, 9 June 2025 (https://thespectator.com/topic/steve-bannon-la-riots-world-war-three/?utm_source=Spectator%20World%20Signup&utm_campaign=12fd9564f8-EMAIL_CAMPAIGN_2025_06_09_08_03&utm_medium=email&utm_term=0_-12fd9564f8-154695757).

11. Diana Hernández, 'What is "Szon Patrol"? New viral trend in Poland puts girls and young women at risk', *Heraldo USA*, 18 September 2025 (https://www.heraldousa.com/opinion/What-is-Szon-Patrol-New-Viral-Trend-in-Poland-Puts-Girls-and-Young-Women-at-Risk-20250918-0022.htmloogle_vignette).

12. Wikipedia, 'Marko Perković' (https://en.wikipedia.org/wiki/Marko_Perkovi%C4%87).

13. Gideon Levy, 'Sanctioning Ben-Gvir and Smotrich is but a tiny, sad step in ending the Gaza massacre', *Haaretz*, 11 June 2025 (https://www.haaretz.com/opinion/2025-06-11/ty-article-opinion/.premium/sanctioning-ben-gvir-and-smotrich-is-but-a-tiny-sad-step-in-ending-the-gaza-massacre/00000197-6063-d34b-ad97-f06beb7d0000).

14. Bhavika Rathore, 'Israeli content creators mock children of Gaza in viral new trend on TikTok', *Hindustan Times*, 6 March 2025 (https://www.hindustantimes.com/world-news/us-news/israeli-content-creators-mock-children-of-gaza-in-viral-new-trend-on-tiktok-watch-101741280809804.html).

15. Yohannes Lowe and Vicky Graham, 'UK politics – Scale of "Unite the Kingdom" march shows free speech "alive and well" in UK, says minister – as it happened', *The Guardian*, 14 September 2025 (https://www.theguardian.com/politics/live/2025/sep/14/unite-the-kingdom-march-tommy-robinson-peter-mandelson-labour-deputy-leader-uk-politics-live-news-updates).

16. Stephen Collinson, 'Trump will never change, but Kirk's death shines a path to MAGA's future', CNN, 22 September 2025 (https://edition.cnn.com/2025/09/22/politics/trump-kirk-vance-funeral-analysis).

17. Quoted from Jeremy Matthew Glick, 'Put Some Red on It: Maoist Brooding and Communist Laughter', *PMLA/Publications of the*

Modern Language Association of America, September 2025, 140(2): 334–342 (https://www.researchgate.net/publication/395161530_Put_Some_Red_on_It_Maoist_Brooding_and_Communist_Laughter).

18. Personal communication.

Donald Trump as a Gramscian

1. Antonio Gramsci, *Quaderni del Carcere*, vol. 1, Quaderni 1–5 (Turin: Giulio Einaudi, editor, 1977), p. 311. English translation quoted from *Selections from the Prison Notebooks of Antonio Gramsci* (London: Lawrence & Wishart, 1971), p. 276.

2. Personal communication.

3. Paul Leslie, 'From Philosophy To Power', *Salmagundi* 226–227, spring/summer 2025 (https://salmagundi.skidmore.edu/articles/1176-from-philosophy-to-power).

4. Gideon Levy, 'Sanctioning Ben-Gvir and Smotrich is but a tiny, sad step in ending the Gaza massacre', *Haaretz*, 11 June 2025 (https://www.haaretz.com/opinion/2025-06-11/ty-article-opinion/.premium/sanctioning-ben-gvir-and-smotrich-is-but-a-tiny-sad-step-in-ending-the-gaza-massacre/00000197-6063-d34b-ad97-f06beb7d0000).

5. Katherine Dee, 'The internet has turned us all into accidental witches', *The Spectator: World* (https://thespectator.com/topic/internet-turned-accidental-witches-charlie-kirk-jezebel/?utm).

6. Wikipedia, 'Murder of George Floyd' (https://en.wikipedia.org/wiki/Murder_of_George_Floyd).

7. Patrick Timmons, Martin Hodgson and David Agren, 'Shocking photo of drowned father and daughter highlights migrants' border peril', *The Guardian*, 26 June 2019 (https://www.theguardian.com/us-news/2019/jun/25/photo-drowned-migrant-daughter-rio-grande-us-mexico-border).

8. TOI desk, '"Ban phones in Jewish schools": Obama's former speechwriter claims Gaza images make defending Israel "impossible"', *The Times of India*, 23 November 2025 (https://timesofindia.indiatimes.com/world/us/ban-phones-in-jewish-schools-obamas-former-speechwriter-says-alleges-gaza-images-make-defending-israel-impossible/articleshow/125511649.cms).

9. Did not something similar happen after Luigi Mangione was arrested on 9 December 2024 and charged with murder in the fatal shooting

of UnitedHealthcare CEO Brian Thompson? (See Kevin Shalvey, Aaron Katersky, Emily Shapiro, Josh Margolin and Meredith Deliso, 'UnitedHealthcare CEO shooting latest: Luigi Mangione has been charged with murder', ABC News, 10 December 2024, https://abcnews.go.com/US/unitedhealthcare-ceo-shooting-latest-net-closing-suspect-new/story?id=116591169.) Although people generally condemned his act, something unexpected happened. UnitedHealthcare was well known for refusing to pay its clients the insurance money they deserved, so Brian Thompson was perceived as a symbol of big companies which ruthlessly profit from small people, and this triggered a large wave of sympathy for Mangione, a wave which went across the usual party divisions. As in the case of Bernie, Mangione became a symbol of the oppressed in the class struggle – a proof that class struggle is lurking beneath the official political lines of division, unable to express itself adequately within the existing political co-ordinates and waiting to explode when opportunity arises.

Mamdani's Wager

1. Emma Brockes, 'Zohran Mamdani's biggest threat is not Donald Trump, it's the Democratic old guard', *The Guardian*, 6 November 2025 (https://www.theguardian.com/commentisfree/2025/nov/06/zohran-mamdani-new-york-democrats-donald-trump).
2. I owe this idea to Alenka Zupančič (personal communication).
3. Sean Seddon and Stuart Lau, 'Elon Musk says he is launching a new political party', BBC, 5 July 2025 (https://www.bbc.com/news/articles/c1dn04lvgpdo).

Conclusion: Abandon All Hope, You Who Enter Radical Politics

1. Quoted from Harold Alderman, et al., 'Heidegger and Nazism', *Journal of the American Political Science Association*, September 1991, 96(2), accessed via researchgate.net (https://www.researchgate.net/publication/249209399_Heidegger_and_Nazism).
2. See Wikipedia, '*The Zone of Interest* (film)' (https://en.wikipedia.org/wiki/The_Zone_of_Interest_(film)).

NOTES

3. Hanns-Georg Rodek, '"The Zone of Interest" and us – a German critique of the provocative Oscar nominee', *WorldCrunch*, 7 March 2024 (https://worldcrunch.com/culture-society/the-zone-of-interest-germany/).

4. Information given to me by Božidar Jezernik of the Philosophical Faculty, University of Ljubljana.

5. See Remi Adekoya's outstanding *It's Not About Whiteness, It's About Wealth* (London: Constable, 2023).

6. Karl Marx, 'Critique of the Gotha Programme', written April or early May 1875, accessed via marxists.org (https://www.marxists.org/archive/marx/works/1875/gotha/).

7. Hanif Kureishi, *Shattered* (London: Penguin, 2024), p. 105.

8. Jorge Semprun, *The Long Voyage* (Los Angeles: Overlook TP, 2005), p. 172.

9. Otto Paans, 'Professional philosophy's failed revolution', *Against Professional Philosophy* blog, 13 February 2017 (https://againstprofphil.org/2017/02/13/professional-philosophys-failed-revolution/).

10. Louis Antoine de Saint-Just, 'Rapport sur les factions de l'étranger', in *Œuvres complètes* (Paris: Gallimard, 2004), p. 695.

11. Jean-Claude Milner, 'The Prince and the Revolutionary', *Crisis and Critique*, 3, 1 (2016): 71–78.

12. Ali Bianco, 'Trump floats sending Americans to foreign prisons. Civil rights groups say that would be illegal', *Politico*, 21 March 2025 (https://www.politico.com/news/2025/03/21/trump-foreign-prison-threats-civil-rights-groups-027162).

13. Albert Kuzor, 'Ghana, Serbia to sign labour mobility agreement as bilateral ties deepen', *Joy Online*, 17 July 2025 (https://www.myjoyonline.com/ghana-serbia-to-sign-labour-mobility-agreement-as-bilateral-ties-deepen/).

14. I owe this idea to a conversation with Nico Graack.

15. Ali Mirchi, Amir AghaKouchak, Kaveh Madani and Mojtaba Sadegh, 'Iran's president calls for moving its drought-stricken capital amid a worsening water crisis – how Tehran got into water bankruptcy', *The Conversation*, 1 December 2025 (https://theconversation.com/irans-president-calls-for-moving-its-drought-stricken-capital-amid-a-worsening-water-crisis-how-tehran-got-into-water-bankruptcy-270456).

Index

Numbers in italics indicate figures.

Adekoya, Remi 146
Adorno 150
Afghanistan 59, 156
Africa Corps 67–68
African National Congress (ANC) 42
Afrika Korps 67–68
Agamben, Giorgio 151
AI 23–24, 26, 152, 157
   algorithms 110
   bots 109–110
   capitalist 8
   FactFinder AI 110
   generative 81, 107, 109
   hasbara 109–110
   OpenAI 24
   post-human 111
   rise of 8–9, 23, 85, 132–133
   scamming 30
Air India Flight 171 9–10
Ajax and Maccabi football match 50
Alice in Wonderland (Carroll) 148
Aloni, Udi 73
Altman, Sam 24
Altona 17–22
Amazon 7, 26, 80, 127
American Utopia, An (Jameson) 84
Amini, Mahsa 21, 41
ANC *see* African National Congress
anti-Semitism 12, 19, 137
Arendt, Hannah 88
Aronowitz, Stanley 84
Assad regime 25

Assange, Julian 59
Ayalon, Ami 73, 91

Badiou, Alain 147
   True Life 8
bai lan 37, 39–40
Baković, Zorana 25
Balfour, Arthur 68
Balfour Declaration 68
Balibar, Etienne 146–147
Ballal, Hamdan 97–98
Bannon, Steve 19, 21–22, 80, 82, 127, 141
Barghouti, Marwan 44, 77–78, 89–91
Bass, Karen 80
Bastille 49
BBC (British Broadcasting Corporation) 4
BDSM 26
Beggar's Opera, The (Gay) 78
Belgrade protests 38–39
Ben-Gvir, Itamar 28, 71, 89–90, 129, 136–137
Benedict XVI (Pope) 129
Benjamin, Walter 7–8, 133, 135, 149
   Jetzt-Zeit 8
Bergson, Henri 124
   The Two Sources of Morality and Religion 124
Bezos, Jeff 26, 104
Biden, Joe 24, 71, 83, 139–140, 141
Big Beautiful Bill 57

INDEX

Big Tech 80, 127
black hats 128
black humour 53, 69
Black Lives Matter 100
black market, weapons 120
Black racial groups 6
   Americans 42
     murder by 125–126
     murder of 137
blackmail 63, 117
Boers 40
Bolsheviks 19, 46
Brecht, Bertolt 78
Bretton Woods 97
Brockes, Emma 141
Brownshirts *see* Sturmabteilung

capitalist dynamic 4
Carroll, Lewis, *Alice in Wonderland* 148
Catholics, traditional 19
Chamberlain, Neville 75
Chauvin, Derek 137–138
Chesterton, G.K., 'The Sign of the Broken Sword' 54–55
China 2, 4–5, 37–44
   AI 26
   bai lan 37, 39
   DeepSeek 23–26
   and European Union 12
   Foreign Minister 12–13
   free market 25
   Great Leap Forward 23
   and Japan 132
   and Myanmar 30
   Tiananmen Square 24–25
   United States collaboration 117–118
   United States tariffs 59, 75–76
   urbanization 21
Christianity, Georg Wilhelm Friedrich Hegel 65
Christians
   evangelical 19
   fundamentalists 4

City University of New York (CUNY) 84
Clausewitz, Carl von 79, 116
Clinton, Bill 1
CNN (Cable News Network) 28, 75–76
Cold War ideologies 25
commodification 26
Communism 3
   ersatz-Communism 7
   Karl Marx 8
Communist countries, steel production 23
Communist vision 6–7
Confucius 10
conservatism 1
   moderate 153
conservative modernization 4
conservative nationalism 33, 36
   Slovenia 34
Conservative Party 33, 131, 143–144
conservative populism 149
Corbyn, Jeremy 131, 143–144
   Our Party 131, 143
Courage of Hopelessness, The (Žižek) 151
Critique of the Gotha Program (Marx) 147
Croatia, Prime Minister 129
CUNY *see* City University of New York
Cuomo, Andrew 141

da Vinci, Leonardo, *The Last Supper* 32
Davis School District 100
de-commodification 23–27
Deadpool 31
decolonization 28–36
DeepSeek 23–26
Deleuze, Gilles 74
Democritus 10–11
Descartes, Rene 9, 32
Devil 65
dominance (AI boom) 23
dominance (BDSM) 26
dominance (Hamas) 71

INDEX

Dow Index 76
DuBois, W. E. B. 53
Dugin, Aleksandr 35–36

East European Jews 68, 76
Eastern Europe 68
Egypt 66, 70–71, 77, 156
elections
    democratic 85
    Gaza 91
    Japan 150
    Palestinian 77
    Reform UK 132
    USA 35, 83–84, 143, 149, 154
Eliot, T. S., *Notes Towards a Definition of Culture* 153
Enlightenment Lite 149
enslavement 8–9, 95, 103–104
Erdogan, Recep Tayyip 4
Eritrea 29
ersatz-Communism 7
Escobar, Pepe 35
Euripides
    Hippolytus 64
    Medea 64
Eurocentrism 125
Europe
    autonomy 57
    civilization 42
    colonizers of 7
    Eurocentric societies 7
    and Gaza 54, 108
    Group of Seven (G7) 17
    heads of state 120
    Israel support 69
    Kurds 42–43
    legacy of 32, 43
    multiculturalism 123
    Palestinian state 66, 90, *90*, 91
    and United States 102, 117–118, 123
European Convention for the Prevention of Torture and Inhuman or Degrading Treatment or Punishment 82
European countries 54, 57
    non-European countries 133
European Union
    and China 12
    Commission President 40
European wars
    defence spending 57
    rearmament 105
    Ukraine *see* Ukraine–Russia war
    World War II *see* Nazism
evangelical Christians 19
ewiger Frieden 134

Facebook 48, 80, 127
FactFinder AI 110
Farage, Nigel 131, 143–144
    Reform UK 131–132, 143
Finkelstein, Norman, *I'll Burn That Bridge* 53
Floyd, George 137–138
French Revolution 49
Freud, Sigmund 20–21, 34, 86
    Unbehagen in der Kultur 35

GAFAM *see* Google, Amazon, Facebook, Apple and Microsoft
Ganz, John 120
gay
    LGBT 1, 3, 33, 100, 123, 132
    super soldiers 60
Gay, John, *The Beggar's Opera* 78
Gaza 63–69, 86–91, 109–121
    governance of 77
    Israeli leafleting 108
    Palestinian treatment in 53–54, 70–71
    reconstruction of 71–72, 74
    Truth Social videos 107–108
Gdansk 7
GDR *see* German Democratic Republic
Georgia 40
German Democratic Republic (GDR) 1, 152

INDEX

Germany 145–157
   Altona 17–22
   Chancellor 17
   Nazi Germany 68, 105, 116, 131, 134
Ghana 152
Girard, Rene 136
Glaucon 11
Glazer, Jonathan, *The Zone of Interest* 145–148
Global South 31
Goebbels, Joseph 18, 128
Goethe, Johann Wolfgang von 8–9, 133
Goldberg, Jonah 1–2
   Liberal Fascism 1
Google 48, 80, 127
Google, Amazon, Facebook, Apple and Microsoft (GAFAM) 4
Graham, Lindsey 118–119
Gramsci, Antonio 19, 130, 136
   populist Gramscians 19–20
   Prison Notebooks 135
Greenland 74
Group of Seven (G7) summit 2025, Israel 17
Guevara, Che 154
Guidance Patrol 41

Haaretz 66, 136
Halevy, Efraim 73
Hamas
   ceasefire 75, 77, 134
   destruction of 66
   Gaza dominance 71
   Iran instigated attacks 17
   Israel financing of 66, 71
   Israel focus on 55
   Israel kibbutz attack 65–66, 138
   Russian arrests 61
   Truth Social video 107
   violence by 74
Han-Pira, Eric 112
Harari, Yuval Noah 56
Harris, Kamala 35

hasbara 109–110
Hegel, Georg Wilhelm Friedrich 114, 139
   Christianity 65
   concrete universality 8, 128, 138
   dialectical progress 11
   Science of Logic 11–12
   Sitten 118
hegemony 136–137, 139, 141
   ideological 19, 130, 136
   United States 97, 99
Hegseth, Pete 80–1, 83
Heidegger, Martin 145
Hewart, Lord 49
Hezbollah 17
Hippolytus (Euripides) 64
Hitler, Adolf
   assassination plot 151
   and Chamberlain 75, 79
   and Goebbels 18
   Jewish blessing 60
   Western sympathizers 17
   and Yevgeny Prigozhin 67
Hollywood, totalitarian aesthetics 1
Horkheimer, Max 1, 150
Höss, Rudolf 145
Houthis 17
Hungary, Prime Minister 32, 36
Hurwitz, Sarah 138
Hussein, Saddam 42–43

Ide, Wendy 32
ideological hegemony 19, 130, 136
IDF *see* Israel Defense Forces
I'll Burn That Bridge (Finkelstein) 53
indigenous peoples 6
Iran 17–18, 21, 134, 154–156
   and Gaza 108
   and Israel 57–58, 134
   Kurds 41–43
   Mahsa Amini protests 41
   President 154
   Revolutionary Guard 155
   and United States 18, 57–59, 76, 134

INDEX

Iraq 40, 42–43
Islamic State of Iraq and Syria (ISIS) 42–43, 61
Israel
   Arab neighbours 21
   Benjamin Netanyahu 109, 134
   diplomacy 109–110, 129
   Finance Minister 71, 129, 136–137
   G7 statement 17
   genocidal logic 55, 78
   hardliners 61, 77
   Jewish supremacy 56
   massacres support 136–137
   Middle East war 65–66, 70–71
   military 28, 108
   Minister of National Security 71
   Mossad 73
   prisoners in 44, 74, 77
   self-defence 40
   two-state solution 66, 77, 91
   United States support of 18–19, 71, 73–74, 155
   Zionist extremists 60, 71, 77, 137
Israel Defense Forces (IDF)
   brutality by 59, 74, 97
   defence of 49
   religious war 66
   threats to 28
   West Bank 66
Israel/Gaza
   academics opposition 50
   ethnic cleansing 68, 71
   genocide 12, 17
   propaganda 130, 133, 138
Israel/Hamas
   ceasefire 75, 77, 134
   financing of 66, 71
   focus 55
   hostages 74
   kibbutz attack 65–66, 138
Israel/Iran 57–58, 134
Israel/Palestinians 53–55, 73
   West Bank occupation 68, 78, 89, 97, 110

Jameson, Fredric 84–85
   An American Utopia 84
Japan, and China 132
Japanese House of Councillors 150
Jetzt-Zeit 8
Johnson, Boris 144
Jolly, Thomas 32, 36
Jones, Owen 59, 109, 116
Jordan 70–71
jouissance 58
Judgement, The (Kafka) 122–123
Jünger, Ernst 61–62

Kafka, Franz, *The Judgement* 122–123
Kant, Immanuel 33
kasha 45
Kerensky, Alexander 46–47
King, Martin Luther 42
King, Stephen, *The Shining* 20
Kirk, Charlie 126–127, 132
Kissinger, Henry 120
KK Park 29
Kravtsova, Vera 29
Kueng, J. Alexander 137–138
Kurdish–Turkish conflict 40
Kurdistan 42
Kurdistan Workers' Party (PKK) 40–41, 43–44
Kurds 41–43
Kureishi, Hanif 147

Labour Party 131, 143–144
Lacan, Jacques 11, 18, 20
   big Other 118, 130
   empty speech 111
   superego 73
   truth 107–108
Lane, Thomas 137
Laos 29
LAPD *see* Los Angeles Police Department
Last Supper, The (da Vinci) 32
Le Pen, Marine 125
Left 1, 137, 139, 141
   anarchic 39

INDEX

change 2
   failure of 6–7, 125
   liberal 2, 102, 126, 150
   modern 41, 53, 127
   populism 80, 84
   radical 3, 35, 84, 150, 153
   threats to 132
   woke 100–101
Leftist 2–3, 135
   democracy 55, 146, 149
   Kurds 43
   parties 131, 143
   radical 144
   totalitarianism 2–3
   utopia 84
   Western 41
   youth 4
Lenin, Vladimir 5, 46–47, 97, 152–153
Levi-Strauss, Claude 7
Levy, Gideon 66, 129, 136
Levy, Henri 133
Levy, Shawn 32
Leyen, Ursula von der 40
LGBT 1, 3, 33, 100, 123, 132
liberal fascism 4–13
Liberal Fascism (Goldberg) 1
Libya 29
Lippmann, Walter, *Public Opinion* 96
Los Angeles
   Mayor of 80
   riots 19
Los Angeles Police Department
   (LAPD) 80
Luxemburg, Rosa 5, 53

McGowan, Todd 135
McNaughton, John, *Wild Things* 63–64
Macron, Emmanuel 116
MAGA (Make America Great Again) 18–19, 57, 96
Magic Mountain, The (Mann) 35
Malaparte, Curzio, *The Technique of Coup d'Etat* 47
Mamdani, Zohran 28, 135, 141–142, 144, 154

Mann, Thomas 34–35
   Reflections of a Nonpolitical Man 34
   The Magic Mountain 35
Mao Zedong 114, 150, 153
Marcuse, Herbert 145
Marie Antoinette 33–34
Markov, Sergei 60
Marshall Plan 96
Marx, Groucho 138
Marx, Karl 8, 31, 147
   Communism 8
   Critique of the Gotha Program 147
Marxism 150, 153
Marxists 5, 26, 46, 80, 135
Matrix, The 110
'Me Too' movement 41
Medea (Euripides) 64
meden 11
Medvedev, Dmitry 113
Meloni, Giorgia 125
Merz, Friedrich 17
Middle East 4–5, 12, 17, 28, 57
   adversaries 57
   Israel war 65, 75, 78, 83, 133–134
Milner, Jean-Claude 99, 101–102, 111, 133
Milošević, Slobodan 38, 78, 131
Minister of National Security 71
Modi, Narendra 4
Morgan, Piers 88
Mormons 100
Mossad 73
Munchhausen, Baron 96
Munich: The Edge of War 151
Murakami, Ryu 4
Musk, Elon 7, 99
   Gaza 107
   Starbase 22
   techno-Trumpism 79
   Teslas 107, 152
   The American Party 143
   and United Kingdom 104
   woke 131
   X 143

INDEX

Muslim Brotherhood 71
Muslim fundamentalists 133
Myanmar 29–30, 154–155

nakhba 72
national security agencies (NSA) 48
Navalny, Alexei 59
Nazi Germany 68, 105, 116, 131, 134
    Schutzstaffel (SS) 98, 148
    Sturmabteilung (SA) 98
Nazi Holocaust 7, 60, 68, 78, 145–146
Nazis 19, 31, 61, 98, 147
    genocide 68, 148–149
    links with 67–68
    neo-Nazi 67, 128
    see also Goebbels, Joseph; Hitler, Adolf
Nazism 98
    Schindler's List (Spielberg) 149
Netanyahu, Benjamin
    and Donald Trump 107, 109, 134
    Gaza destruction 67
    Gaza displacement 53
    and Iran 155
    Israel expansion 89, 134
    war criminal label 78
New Amsterdam 85
New Economic Policy (NEP) 5
Newsom, Gavin 80, 82
Nobel Peace Prize 89, 134
North Atlantic Treaty Organization (NATO) 57
    countries 125
    defence spending 57
    Secretary General 57
    territory 123
North Korea 59, 114, 152
Norwood, Tilly 81
Notes Towards a Definition of Culture (Eliot) 153
Novi Sad 38–39
NSA *see* national security agencies

Obama, Barack 82
Obama, Michelle 138

Ocalan, Abdullah 40–41, 43
October Revolution 45, 48–49
On Dialectical and Historical Materialism (Stalin) 5
OpenAI 24
Orban, Viktor 32, 36
Ottoman region 68
Our Party 131, 143

Paans, Otto 149–150
Palestinian Authority 28, 91
Palestinians 17, 54–56, 58
    fate of 74, 107, 109
    Gaza 66, 69, 70–72, 78, 116
    genocide 79, 88
    and Israel 68, 73, 77, 91, 133–134
    and Jews 78
    and United States 66, 71, 77–78
    West Bank 28, 66
Panama 74
Paris Olympics 31–35
Paris protests 6, 39
Pentagon 81
Perković, Marko 128–129
Peshmerga 43
Peters, Stephen 64
Philosophers' Steamers 5
Pišek, Mojca 126
PKK *see* Kurdistan Workers' Party
Plato 11
    The Republic 11–12
Platonists
    anti-Platonists 11
    sophists 11
Plenković, Andrej 129
poiesis 133
Poland
    Gdansk 7
    Schindler's List (Spielberg) 149
    Szon Patrol 127–128
Polemarchus 11
polis 9
political correctness 1, 34, 99
Pontius Pilate 65
populist Gramscians 19–20

INDEX

Postcolonial Volk, The (Zacharias) 30
POTUS *see* President of the United States
praxis 133
President of China 1–2
President of Croatia 78
President of the EU Commission 40
President of Iran 154
President of Russia
    Dmitry Medvedev 113
    Vladimir Putin *see* Putin, Vladimir
President of Serbia
    Aleksandar Vučić 38–40
    Slobodan Milošević 38, 78, 131
President of Turkey 4
President of Ukraine *see* Zelensky, Volodymyr
President of the United States (POTUS) 117
    Barack Obama 82
    Bill Clinton 1
    Donald Trump *see* Trump, Donald
    Joe Biden 24, 71, 83, 139–140, 141
    Oval Office 113–116, 118–119
Prigozhin, Yevgeny 67–68
Prime Minister of India 4
Prison Notebooks (Gramsci) 135
Proud Boys 61–62
Provisional Government, Russia 46
Public Opinion (Lippmann) 96
Putin, Vladimir 1–2, 4
    and Donald Trump 58–59, 75, 76, 86–87, *87*, 88
    European Convention withdrawal 81–82
    European multiculturalism 123
    and Tucker Carlson 119
    Ukraine war 79, 116

Qatar 58, 66, 76
Quantico 80
Quran 109

Ramirez, Oscar 138
Ramirez, Valeria 138

Red Guards 46–47
Red Square 112
Reflections of a Nonpolitical Man (Mann) 34
Reform UK 131–132, 143
Reijn, Halina, *Babygirl* 26–27
Republic, The (Plato) 11–12
Revolutionary Guard 155
Right, populist 2
Robeson, Paul 53
Rodek, Hanns-Georg 146
Rommel, Erwin 67
Roosevelt, Franklin Delano 96, 105, 132
Roosevelt New Deal 96
Rothschild, Lord 68
Roy, Arundhati 56
RT (formerly Russia Today) 61
Rubio, Marco 117
Russia 1–2, 45–50, 122–134
    Bolsheviks 19, 46
    October Revolution 45, 48–49
    Provisional Government 46
    Red Guards 46–47
    Red Square 112
    Ukraine *see* Ukraine–Russia war
    Winter Palace Petrograd 45–46
    see also Lenin, Vladimir; Putin, Vladimir; Soviet Union; Stalin, Joseph; Trotsky, Leon
Rutte, Mark 57–58

SA *see* Sturmabteilung
Safiya, Abu 77–78
Sahin, Idris Naim 103
Samsung 7
Sanders, Bernie 127, 139, *139*, 141–142, 144
Saudi Arabia 42, 77
Schindler's List (Spielberg) 149
Schutzstaffel (SS) 98, 148
Science of Logic (Hegel) 11–12
Semprun, Jorge 148
Senate 95
Serbia 4, 37–40, 78, 131, 152

INDEX

Belgrade protests 38–39
   president of 38
Shin Bet 73, 91, 110
Shining, The (King) 20
Shklovsky, Viktor 45
Shoah 69, 149
'Sign of the Broken Sword, The'
   (Chesterton) 54–55
Simonyan, Margarita 61
slavery 6, 29
Sloterdijk, Peter 53
Slovenia, conservative nationalism 34
Smithsonian Institution 99
Smotrich, Bezalel 71, 129, 136–137
social order, traditionalist 4
Socrates 8–11, 24, 45
South Africa, Boers 40
South Korea 7, 152
Soviet Union 17, 23, 112, 145
   see also Russia
Spartans 60
Spielberg, Steven, *Schindler's List* 149
Spinoza, Baruch 8
SS *see* Schutzstaffel
Stalin, Joseph 150
   and Donald Trump 83, 111, 114
   On Dialectical and Historical Materialism 5
   oppression 5
   purges 99, 111
   statue 60
Stalinism 135, 151
   and Cancel Culture 113
   enforced happiness 74
   factual truth 111–112
   language 112
Stalinist Party 84
Starlink 30
Starmer, Keir 78, 116
Sturmabteilung (SA) 98
sub species actualtatis 8
sub species aeternitatis 8
Sudan 29, 66, 86, 154
Sultana, Zarah, Our Party 131, 143
sumud 71–72, 74

Syria 25, 40, 42–43, 61, 120
Szon Patrol 127–128

Tacitus 67
Taiwan 2, 24
Taliban 59
Tamkin, Emily 19
Tang ping 37
Technique of Coup d'Etat, The
   (Malaparte) 47
Teslas 107, 152
Thailand 29–30
Theroux, Louis 89
Theweleit, Klaus 64
Thiel, Peter 99, 136
Third Way liberal Left 150
Third World 35, 150
Thorburn, John 64
Tiananmen Square 24–25
Tomer-Yerushalmi, Major General
   Yifat 28
traditional Catholics 19
Trotsky, Leon 46–49
   United Trotskyite-Zinovievite
   Centre 112
True Life (Badiou) 8
Trump, Donald
   and Andrew Cuomo 141
   and Charlie Kirk 126, 132
   and Democratic Party 142, 144
   dictatorial style 95
   diplomatic style 118
   elections 2019 83
   and Elon Musk 79
   and Franklin D. Roosevelt 96, 132
   and Gavin Newsom 80
   and God 1–3, 57, 80, 83, 103
   ideology of 98–102, 152–153
   impeachment 142
   and Joseph Stalin 83, 111, 113–114
   and religion 54
   and Republican Party 142
   and sexism 32, 118
   and Vladimir Putin 59, 75, 76,
   86–87, 87, 88

INDEX

and Volodymyr Zelensky 58, 113–116, 119–121
and Zohran Mamdani 141–142
Trump, Donald administration
  armed forces discipline 82–83
  Big Beautiful Bill 57
  Big Tech 80, 127
  freedom in 104
  Los Angeles riots 19
  National Guard 83
  neofascism 4, 149
  policy shifting 110
  realists 120
  replacement of 98–99
  tactics of 96–97
Trump, Donald, AI
  DeepSeek 23–24
  executive orders 24
Trump, Donald, foreign policy
  Africa 126
  China 59, 75–76, 117–118
  European Union 102, 117–118, 123
  Greenland 74
  Kurds 42
  marine deployment 80
  NATO 57–58
  Palestine 66, 71, 77–78
  Panama 74
  tariffs 97
  trade wars 75–76
  United Kingdom 18–19, 58
  United Nations 18, 123
Trump, Donald as peacemaker; Gaza 58
  governance of 77
  Israeli leafleting 108
  Palestinian treatment in 70–71
  reconstruction of 71–72, 74
  Truth Social videos 107–108
Trump, Donald as peacemaker; Iran 18, 134
  Israel ceasefire 57–58
  negotiations with 59
  Qatar strikes 76
  threats against 58

Trump, Donald as peacemaker; Israel
  Benjamin Netanyahu 107, 109, 134
  genocidal logic 55, 78
  Iran ceasefire 57–58
  Israel/Hamas ceasefire 75, 77, 134
Trump, Donald as peacemaker;
  Ukraine *see* Ukraine–Russia war
Trump, Donald, and populism 2–4, 8, 132, 140
  alternative to 84
  foreign intruders 21–22
  and liberal democracy 102
  MAGA isolationism 18, 96
  Proud Boys 61–62
  Rightist populism 17–18, 135–136, 142–143
  rise of 125
  superego 73
Truth Social 76, 107–108
Truthout 76
Tsemel, Lea 98
Tudjman, Franjo 78
Turk, Žiga 34
Turkey 4, 40–44, 77, 156
  minister of the interior 103
Two Sources of Morality and Religion, The (Bergson) 124

Ukraine 123, 154–155
  China view of 13
  crime in 49
  violence in 66
  Volodymyr Zelensky *see* Zelensky, Volodymyr
Ukraine–Russia war 79, 82, 114, 116
  Armed Forces 60
  drone attacks 59, 155
  Europe role 76, 123
  gay super soldiers 60
  justification of 67
Ukraine–Russia war, Trumpian politics 12–13
  arms restrictions 59
  arms to 76

INDEX

economic interests 119
natural resources 70, 119
peace negotiations 35, 79, 134
Putin talks 59, 86–87
Ukraine pressure 58–59, 75–76, 83
unjust peace 79
UN *see* United Nations
United Arab Emirates 77
United Kingdom 3
 central shift 125
 Conservative Party 33, 131, 143
 and Donald Trump 19, 58
 and Elon Musk 131
 Labour Party 131, 143–144
 liberalism 3
 Our Party 131, 143
 Palestinian state 66
 Prime Minister 78, 116, 144
 protests 130–131
 Reform UK 131–132, 143
 tariffs 58
 US–UK trade deal 18–19
United Nations
 General Assembly 12, 123
 peacemaker 18
 Special Rapporteur 82
 State of Israel 68
United States 18, 57, 75–85, 95–106, 135–140
 army 83
 Federal law 99
 hegemony 97, 99
 Marshall Plan 96
 Roosevelt New Deal 96
 US–UK trade deal 18–19
 US–USSR Space Race 23
United States Congress 95–96, 117
United States Democratic Party 82, 142, 14
 Kamala Harris 35
 Michelle Obama 138
United States Democratic Socialists 141, 143–144
 Bernie Sanders 127, 139, *139*, 141–142, 144

United States National Guard 80, 83, 141
United States Pentagon 81
United States presidential elections
 1952 84
 2019 83
 2024 35
United States Republican Party
 establishment 141–144
 hawks 18
 Lindsey Graham 118–119
 and MAGA isolationists 18
United States Senate 95
United States Supreme Court powers 57
United States The American Party 143
United Trotskyite-Zinovievite Centre 112
Utah Parents United 100

Vance, J. D.
 character of 99
 diplomatic style 113–115, 119
 and Donald Trump 98–99
 Munich Security Conference 102
 and Peter Thiel 99, 136
 and Volodymyr Zelensky 58, 113–116, 119–121
Varoufakis, Yanis 25–26, 97, 102
Vaturi, Nissim 109
Velikiye Lukim 60
völkisch 31
Vučić, Aleksandar 38–40

Wagner Group 67–68
Wagner, Richard 35
Wall Street 97
Walmart 80, 127
Wang Yi 12–13
Weiss, Daniella 88–89, 91
western Europe 3–4, 54, 66, 90, 125
 leaders 87
White House 58, 107, 110, 113–114, 118, 127, 142–143
Wild Things (McNaughton) 63–64

INDEX

Winter Palace Petrograd 45–46
Wisman, Heinz 11
Wittgenstein, Ludwig 11
Wolverine 31
World War II 67, 96–97, 114, 128, 145
World War III 80, 119

X 117, 143
Xi Jinping 1–2
Xiang Biao 21–22

Yarvin, Curtis 126

Zacharias, Benjamin 30–31
   The Postcolonial Volk 30
Zaharova, Marija 113
Zalloua, Zahi 55
Zan, Zendegi, Azadi 41
Zarutska, Iryna 125–126

Zelensky, Volodymyr 87, 110, 117–118
   and J. D. Vance 58, 113–116, 119–121
Zionist 54
   extremists 60
   hasbara 110
   ideology 72, 110
   narratives 68, 110
   neo-fascist 78
   network 59
   radical 77
Zionist Federation of Great Britain and Ireland 68
Zionist Jews 19, 55
Žižek, Slavoj 4
   The Courage of Hopelessness 151
   Žižek's Jokes 4
Zone of Interest, The (Glazer) 145–148
Zoom 7, 155
Zupanèiè, Alenka 18